Did Jesus Wear Undies?

A Parents Guide to Answering
Big Bible Questions for Little Ears

RYAN GENTLES

DEDICATION

This book must be dedicated to my wife, Lindsay. She lets me dream big and go up to the clouds, brings me back down to reality, and encourages me in the right direction. I would not have started or finished this book without her constant encouragement and sacrifice. She not only bore the children that have asked these questions, but she continues to speak the Truth of the Gospel to them.

Thank you, Love!

To my girls, I love you and I am so blessed to have you as my girls! Thank you for asking questions. Thank you for listening to the answers! Please keep asking questions!

FOREWORD

Kids are notorious for asking unexpected questions. Was Jesus potty trained? Does God watch us in the shower? Did Jesus practice walking on the water? They say there are no dumb questions. Seemingly innocent questions usually point to much bigger questions. There is always a greater question behind the question. *Did Jesus Wear Undies?* is profound because it's a clever way kids are wanting to know who is Jesus? and how can they know Him?

During His ministry on earth Jesus asked hundreds of questions. Who do you say that I am? Where is your faith? Do you want to be well? He already knew the answers. His questions are meant for us to discover the answers for ourselves.

In the life of kids, God questions help them find their passion and purpose. Questions are powerful (even the silly ones.) They can spark curiosity, stir the soul and bring about a seismic shift which leads to incredible Ah Ha moments.

The real art of questions that are born in the soul is giving them answers that go beyond the fad-chasing, self-centered, temporary experience of this world.

Being a parent is tough! It's a life lived in the vortex of hustle and hurry. Caught in between the noise and necessity of everything, we get used to the grind. It's hard to see out beyond the hedges with truth and a fresh perspective. The little things often get by us. It's the little things that contain big opportunities.

I'm thankful for Ryan's ability to help us recognize that questions arise in the stuff of ordinary life; studying, playing, eating, shuttling to music recitals, sports, dentist and doctors. Ryan helps us recognize the eternity of the moments and point our conversation toward God.

You'll discover in this book that the questions our kids are asking are the questions that never fade. They demand answers that never fail. The force of *Did Jesus Wear Undies?* is answers. Ryan has provided the scriptural anchors for your children's questions. A well given answer can liberate, empower, deliver, re-energize and reorient a child's way of seeing the world. This book is long enough to provide thoughtful answers and short enough to be used with your kids. Ryan is a fresh theological voice who is able to take big biblical concepts and place them within reach of both parents and kids.

This book provides short, powerful answers for life's biggest questions. Talking to kids about God sized questions is not just about getting it right. Yes, we learn the truth of God, understand the gospel and read scripture. But it's about living it right. We help our kids work out the answers in a world of doubt and deception, rejection and competition.

The book you hold in your hand is not just a book. It's a discipleship tool for you and your family. Before using this book with your family, I suggest you do two things: one, you read it through first. Internalize the answers. Get the content in your heart and mind. Two, in your Bible highlight the scriptures referenced in this book and in the margin, write the question they answer.

As the landscape of our culture continues to shift, it's important we join the conversation by giving our kids timeless answers in turbulent times to help them think and live biblically. I'm thankful for the resource Ryan Gentles has created. Now go give an answer for the hope that is within you.

DAVID EDWARDS
Speaker and Author

INTRODUCTION

I married the love of my life, Lindsay, in 2008. We were so excited to start a family together and get to be parents to some awesome kids! Lindsay gave birth to our first born in 2014 and I got to claim the title "Dad." Lindsay and I have always said that people don't understand their own selfishness until they get married. And then the realization of selfishness hits again when those people have kids. That is one of the blessings most people don't talk about when talking about parenthood.

Please understand that I'm not saying being selfish is a blessing. But rather, recognizing your own selfishness and having that truth exposed is a blessing to encourage you to move away from selfish living. Being a parent will move you one way or the other. I'm glad I am seeing it move me toward selflessness. Note, I didn't say I'm perfectly selfless but rather I am moving toward it.

Here's one way God is helping me in that movement.

Once my beautiful little girls could talk, they all started with question after question. Not all of their questions are about spiritual or biblical things but a good chunk have been over the years. I knew early on that I needed to keep track of those questions because they were good, challenging questions.

One might think that it was a little over dramatic to keep track of toddler questions. How deep could those questions be, right? Well let me tell you, some of these questions take you deep into the cobweb filled pages of your Bibles.

A question that was asked early on really hit me with the idea of writing this book. A asked, "Did God die on the cross?" Well, I didn't want to give her the wrong answer. I didn't want to overload her with information that would confuse her 5-year-old brain. And I didn't want to just blow off the question because she obviously wanted to know the answer. Something I learned early on in parenthood is that kids really want to know the answer. But they also want you to answer how they can understand it! So, I set out to make sure they knew that there is an answer and one way or another, we would talk through it.

THE CHALLENGE

Here's the challenging part of all these questions. My girls started asking questions that were deep and needed some heavy background to answer properly. I have the education and ministry experience to answer the questions. I had been answering these types of questions for years in student ministry and with young adults in church. The challenge was that my girls were young, and I had about two minutes to get the answer to them before they lost interest. Remember, they want to know the answer, but it needs to be quick and in their language.

After realizing this challenge, another rose to the top. I needed to make sure I wasn't teaching them incorrect theological building blocks that I would have to help them break back down later. Something that triggered this thought in me was the reminder of the old rhyme, "Here's the Church."

THE TRIGGER

If you grew up around church or went to a VBS as a kid, you probably heard someone teach this to little kids. You clasp your hands together with your index fingers pointing up like a steeple and the rest of your fingers tucked in the closed hands.

"Here's the church, here's the steeple. Open the door (open your hands and wiggle fingers) And see all the people."

This cute little rhyme sets up our kids with incorrect ecclesiology (study of the church). The building (hands) is not the church. The PEOPLE are God's church, God's bride. We, as the church, have set up generations to say, "I'm going to church." What we really mean is that we are going to a building that the church gathers in for worship or prayer. It may seem trivial and nitpicky, but if we continue down this path with other things, we will have generations that don't understand biblical truths because the foundation they are standing on is wrong. If the **foundation is wrong, we will have to tear it down and rebuild everything.**

I don't want that.

So, I set out to answer my girls' questions as biblically and quickly as possible. No, I didn't have a perfect answer right away for every question. But I did make sure my girls knew I was keeping track of the question and they would get an answer.

WHY DID I WRITE THIS BOOK?

I know I'm not the only parent that hears difficult questions. I know this because friends started sending me the questions from their kids once they found out I was keeping track of my girls' questions. That helps me as a parent to know that I'm in the same boat with so many others.

God has been working in my heart over the last several years dealing with perspectives. I believe one of the perspectives He desires for me to view life through is simple. He wants me to know that I need other parents to come alongside me in parenting. That is what I believe God wants from this book. I want it to be something that comes alongside other parents or adults being asked these questions by kids and be a resource. I want this to be a tool in your toolbelt!

I wrote this book to help you boil down the answers to teach children the Truth of God's Word. This book's intention is to help set you up for success in leading and discipling the children in your life. That can be your children, your grandchildren, or even friends' children that bless you with some influence in their lives. My hope is that this book will be a resource for church bodies to hand to parents in preparation for the tough questions coming or for those amid the questions.

HOW TO USE THIS TOOL

Instructions are great! I am not one of those guys that throws instructions away before I build something. In fact, I want to see the entire route for a trip on my phone before I leave the house! I want to know how it's supposed to be done. That's why I want to show you a glimpse of what you are going to see in this book and how you can use it. Plus, we will discuss how you can be a part of the ongoing conversation when it comes to tough theological questions asked by kids!

The format of each chapter is simple

QUESTION
PARENT TERMS
KID TERMS
WHY IT'S TRUE
REVISIT THE TRUTH

We will just put the question out there. Like I said, simple. And I know you will want to get to the answer as quickly as possible. But I am a firm believer in helping people understand the depth of the question so that the answer will seem simple.

The PARENT TERMS will be the bulk of information for you. There will be some commentary quotes, scripture references, historical background or some other "fill in the gap" information for you. This is not to overwhelm you. It is there for YOUR understanding of the question. Again, the better you understand, the easier to answer. Plus, the information in this section will hopefully spark more questions for you and possibly your children.

The KID TERMS is the simple, quick breakdown. This is geared toward the 5-9 year old. If you skip to this part, it might seem too simple of an answer. The purpose of the PARENT TERMS is to thicken up the answers for the kids. My aim was to give you an answer that could be given in less than two minutes. It should have enough information to keep the conversation going if the child desires.

WHY IT'S TRUE is just that. It's the scripture that supports the terms that are used. This book isn't just my opinion on questions. The hope is that the questions are answered quickly and BIBLICALLY. That's a key point to the book. There will be only a few for some questions and there could be several for others. There isn't a formula for how many verses are needed to cover a question for it to be valid.

The last element of each chapter is the REVISIT THE TRUTH section. Remember, these KID TERMS are aimed at a younger crowd range of 5-9 years old. This section takes you a little deeper into this answer and expounds on more truths that can help in understanding or even link to other questions that come up in the answer. This section is usually pointed at a specific passage that may or may not have already been referenced in the chapter. Please read through this section and use it for those future conversations.

JOIN THE CONVERSATION

One final way you can use this resource to grow and disciple your children is by being a part of the podcast. The purpose of the podcast is to go even deeper into these questions. We will branch off into the questions that stem from the book questions. We will break down some of the content in each chapter to explain more of the why behind the answer. Also, the podcast is a great place where you can submit your own questions! We want this community to come together and know that we are all striving for the same thing: We all want the Truth to be taught to our children.

I hope this book is a great resource for you. I know it has been a huge stretch in my faith writing it and evaluating the answers. Would you please be in prayer as others are struggling to answer questions from kids or even adults about faith and God? We want to be prepared to answer these questions. God doesn't want us prepared because He needs us to be to validate Him, but rather because we are called to be ready. Plus, the more we know about God, the more we can worship about who He is!

Happy reading!

CONNECT WITH ME!

I want to make sure we continue to connect and grow together. Please take a minute and connect with me through email.

Check out the link below.

http://eepurl.com/ia9RZn

I want to be able to keep in touch with you and provide more tools for you in this journey.

You will get emails about things like...

1. FREEBIES!
2. More Questions/Answers to walk through
3. Updates on the Podcast
4. Did I mention Freebies?
5. Info on LIVE events
6. And MUCH MORE!

I CAN'T WAIT TO CONNECT WITH YOU!

CONTENTS

GOD—WHO HE IS AND HIS NATURE

GOD + ME—GODS INTERACTIONS WITH ME IN LIFE AND SALVATION

GOD + CHURCH—HOW GOD
LEADS AND SPEAKS TO HIS CHURCH

GOD—
Who He is and
His nature

DID GOD DIE ON THE CROSS? (If God is God and Jesus is Jesus?)

PARENT TERMS

Driving home from picking up my girls, I hear in the back seat, "Daddy, I have a question." I love conversations that start like that! There are times that it is a silly question, but not today! "Go ahead honey, I'm listening."

"Did God die on the cross?

Beg your pardon? I had to take a second to make sure I heard it correctly.

I was driving in rush hour traffic and I honestly was not ready for a question like that. I was thinking it was going to be a question about dinner or dessert or even about a show they had watched. I wasn't ready to have a trinitarian discussion with my preschool aged children.

But, I didn't want to ignore it or answer it incorrectly to have to break it down later and correct my answer.

The answer I gave: "Yes, because Jesus is fully God."

"But God is God and Jesus is Jesus."

Yes, those are correct statements. We have a triune God.

It is a tricky question. YES. Jesus is God, but God is God and Jesus is Jesus. We have a triune God, The Father, Son and Spirit.

So, the answer I gave, "Yes, because Jesus is fully God."

In Genesis 1, we see the plurality of God's essence in merely his name, *Elohim*. *El* is the singular name of God but *Elohim* is the plural name. God says in Genesis 1:26, "Let *us* make man in our image." He speaks of himself (as well as the writer) in plural form.

John 1:1 takes the point even further when we are introduced to Jesus as The Word.

One thing we need to note in this discussion is that Jesus was fully God, and He was fully man. He walked, He talked, He lived in the same style of houses and ate the same kind of food as everyone else. And it was His humanity that died on the cross. We don't see the essence of God die on the cross. There is a beautiful picture of something called propitiation that happens as the Son is separated from the Father because Jesus becomes sin for us (Gal 3:13). The propitiation is a full atonement, or payment, of a debt. The death of Jesus on the cross is this atonement.

The separation happens because sin cannot exist around God's holy presence and we see Jesus ask, "My God, my God, why have you forsaken me?" Jesus is our propitiation on the cross as our sacrifice to God the Father for payment of our sins. His human death is the only sacrifice that could possibly satisfy the wrath of God. And Jesus was obedient to become the sacrifice needed to restore mankind's relationship with God. So, Jesus maintained His deity while allowing His humanity to die on the cross.

KID TERMS

The answer is yes, but not in the way you might think. Jesus is fully God and man. He took on human form (John 1:14, Hebrews 2:17) to be like us. When Jesus died on the cross, the human part in him died and Jesus was separated from the Father. His divine (Godly) nature, or part, did not die. He lived in a real human body that ate, slept, walked and talked and then died on the cross. His spirit/nature is eternal.

So, who God is as the all-powerful being did not die on the cross that day. We see the human nature that he took on himself die a very painful death for us.

WHY IT'S TRUE

> Genesis 1:26—*"Then God said, "Let us make man in our image, after our likeness."*

God made man in His own image. We are the image bearers of God. He started with Adam and then gave us a new "Adam" in Jesus that would be in the same likeness and image to be the sacrifice needed to redeem us from the curse of the Law.

> John 1:1,14;—1:1 *"In the beginning was the Word, and the Word was with God, and the Word was God."*

> John 1:14—*"And the Word became flesh and dwelt among us, and we have seen his glory, glory as of the only Son from the Father, full of grace and truth."*

> John 10:30—*"I and the Father are one."* This shows us that Jesus is one with the Father and what we know about God is that He has always existed. He is eternal. So, Jesus lived in that divine, eternal state while also taking on flesh and living as a man.

> Hebrews 2:17—*"Therefore he had to be made like his brothers in every respect,*

so that he might become a merciful and faithful high priest in the service of God, to make propitiation for the sins of the people."—Jesus had purpose in becoming flesh. He became like us, he became the high priest we needed, and he became flesh to be the propitiation (atonement) we needed.

REVISIT THE TRUTH

Looking closer at Hebrews 2:17, we see why Jesus took on flesh when he came to earth. He didn't just come from Heaven and start teaching. He became a man in every aspect. This passage says he did this "so that he might become a merciful and faithful high priest in the service of God, to make propitiation for the sins of the people."

The priests were the chosen group to bring the sin offerings to God. Part of that process was for the priest to walk through a purification process prior to bringing the sin offerings of the people so that the offering was not tainted by his sin. This part of the process Jesus did not have to do because He came as the High Priest, perfect before God. And the offering He brought was his own perfect life, bringing an end to the sacrificial system because He completed it on the cross.

5

WHO MADE JESUS?

PARENT TERMS

Jesus was not made. Genesis 1:1 speaks to the plurality of the Godhead. *Elohim* is the name of God in Genesis 1:1 and it is plural. We also see in the translation that God says, "Let us make man," when referring to himself. The plurality of this name changes as God the Father speaks of Himself or of His Son or Spirit.

The "only-begotten" title given to Jesus does not refer to his being physically made. It is the phrase used to signify "only one of its kind". There is no other like him. Jesus did take on human form when he "tabernacled" or dwelt among us (John 1:14) as The Word. And yes, Mary gave birth to him as a baby, but WHO he is and his being has always been. Remember, He was born of a virgin, He does not have an earthly father. He humbled himself and took on flesh.

Colossians 1:15 says that Jesus is the image of the invisible God, the firstborn of all creation. This title of firstborn is pointing to multiple things. The first being his superiority. Jesus is superior overall. The second thing about this title is that it pertains to the birthright, or inheritance, deserved of the "firstborn" and the right that person has to the inheritance. The third thing directs us to the truth that he existed before. His title has always existed as superior because He has always existed.

KID TERMS

One of the mind-blowing things about Jesus is that he wasn't made. He has always been around. It's hard to really understand because we don't know of anything on earth that didn't come from some place or from some thing. But we see in the Bible that Jesus has always existed and that's because he is God.

John 1:1 says, "In the beginning was the Word and the Word was with God, and the Word was God." The Word is Jesus!

It can be confusing because he is called the "firstborn among creation" and His name is the Son of God. What we know is that those names, firstborn and Son, are titles to show us He is in charge. Those names help us to remember that he is also equal with God the Father.

Remember, if he was made, he couldn't be God because God has always been.

WHY IT'S TRUE

> John 1:1—*"In the beginning was the Word, and the Word was with God, and the Word was God"*

John shows us that Jesus (The Word) has always existed and is, in fact, God. This passage can be broken down more in the original language. The semantics of this verse show us that Jesus and God the Father are one in essence but separate persons.

> Colossians 1:15-20—*"He is the image of the invisible God, the firstborn of all creation. For by him all things were created, in heaven and on earth, visible and invisible, whether thrones or dominions or rulers or authorities—all things were created through him and for him. And he is before all things, and in him all things hold together. And he is the head of the body, the church. He is the beginning, the firstborn from the dead, that in everything he might be preeminent. For in him all the fullness of God was pleased to dwell, and through him to reconcile to himself all things, whether on earth or in heaven, making peace by the blood of his cross."*

We see more of a description of who Christ is and that all things have been created by him and for him. So, if he created all things and all things created were created for Him, then He must have existed before all things.

> John 8:58— *"Jesus said to them, 'Truly, truly, I say to you, before Abraham was, I am.'"*

Who made Jesus? According to Him, no one did, and he always has been. This is an outright claim to being God. That is why in the next verse we see people picking up stones to throw at him for what they thought was blasphemy. Jesus has always existed and that is only something God can claim.

REVISIT THE TRUTH

> John 14:9—*Philip asks to see the Father. Jesus's response is "If you have seen me, you have seen the Father."*

That is a bold statement. In fact, if that statement wasn't true, it would be a blasphemous statement for Jesus to make. We see Jesus claim his oneness with the Father throughout the New Testament. Because of this oneness, and distinction in personhood, we begin to see the triune nature of God. When the Spirit is spoken of, we see the language of the

Godhead (Acts 5:3-4, 1 Corinthians 12). These passages help solidify the truth of a triune God which points us back to the question of "Who made Jesus?" No one made Jesus because he is God, and God is the creator and sustainer of all things.

WHY DID JESUS NEED TO DIE?

PARENT TERMS

This question can be expanded to tie into a few other questions (which is what happened in our conversation once this was asked). Couldn't Jesus just have lived a perfect life and told us to do the same? Why didn't Jesus just send a perfect sacrifice, other than himself, and told Israel to sacrifice it for the sins of the world? Why did it have to be Him?

It is a layered question to say the least. Let's start from the top.

Why did Jesus need to die and not simply live a perfect life and go back to Heaven? Well, Hebrews 2 gives us a reason why. He needed to take on flesh and die. One thing to remember is that Jesus' flesh died because Jesus is God and did not have a perishable nature, only a perishable body.

The wages of sin is death. God's standard for justice is much higher than ours. In fact, the standard is perfection, and we cannot reach perfection on our own. In the Old Testament, God instructed His people to provide a sacrifice for the sins that were committed against Him. Even within this design of sacrifice, it has a finite nature. A sacrifice would need to be made later for other sins continuously. Thus, pointing to the necessity of an infinite solution. A solution that only God Himself could overcome for us.

Jesus took on flesh to defeat death. Romans 8:1-4 shows us that Jesus became flesh because the imperfect flesh had weakened the law. For humans, following the law was not going to be good enough. God needed to take on flesh Himself to then condemn the sin in the flesh so that the righteous requirement of the law would be fulfilled in us. He died like mankind to destroy the one who has the power of death. He was made like his brothers in every respect to become a "faithful high priest." (Hebrews 2:17)

This high priest element is huge. Jesus became the perfect high priest that was able to go before God to present the sacrifice for God's people without having to cleanse himself first. He also was the sacrifice because there was and is no other perfect sacrifice available.

Jesus had to become a man in order to be able to die. Jesus had to die to experience all of what mankind experienced so that He could be the merciful and faithful priest He was called to be for us. Before taking on flesh, Jesus did not have flesh and blood to pour out as an offering to God the Father. So, Jesus becoming man is what was needed to provide the necessary sacrifice to God.

Jesus couldn't simply live perfectly and go back to Heaven. God is Just. The payment for sin is a real thing and God must pour out His wrath on sin because He is Just. If we are a follower of Christ, God doesn't ignore our sin or the debt due Him. The wrath due from sin was poured out on Christ on the cross. So, His death is a necessary step for our redemption and for the defeat of death.

KID TERMS

In the Old Testament, God makes a way for His people to pay for their sins for a short time. They would kill animals because God said the payment needed to be a life. We get to serve a God that was willing to be the only acceptable sacrifice to fully pay for our sins. Jesus could have just lived a perfect life and gone back to Heaven. But then we still would have owed God for our sins and Christ would not have completed what He came to earth to do. We'd probably still be killing animals in repentance of our sins.

His death gave us life. It gave us life because God poured His punishment on Christ on the cross for our sins so that He would die, be resurrected, and defeat death for us. That is something that we would never be able to do. That means that Jesus needed to die so we could be saved and redeemed (bought back) with his blood.

13

WHY IT'S TRUE

> Hebrews 2:14-18—*"**14** Since therefore the children share in flesh and blood, he himself likewise partook of the same things, that through death he might destroy the one who has the power of death, that is, the devil, **15** and deliver all those who through fear of death were subject to lifelong slavery. **16** For surely it is not angels that he helps, but he helps the offspring of Abraham. **17** Therefore he had to be made like his brothers in every respect, so that he might become a merciful and faithful high priest in the service of God, to make propitiation for the sins of the people. **18** For because he himself has suffered when tempted, he is able to help those who are being tempted."*

Our high priest destroyed death so that we could have life. He shared in our human form and shared in the sufferings of flesh. This truth humbly brings him to "our level" and places Him on the cross to then render death powerless over the flesh for us.

> Romans 8:1-4—*"There is therefore now no condemnation for those who are in Christ Jesus. **2** For the law of the Spirit of life has set you free in Christ Jesus from the law of sin and death. **3** For God has done what the law, weakened by the flesh,*

could not do. By sending his own Son in the likeness of sinful flesh and for sin, he condemned sin in the flesh, 4 in order that the righteous requirement of the law might be fulfilled in us, who walk not according to the flesh but according to the Spirit."

The law was weakened by the flesh. Christ taking on flesh creates a scenario that could give us a perfect sacrifice in the flesh to atone for sins.

1 John 4:10— *"In this is love, not that we have loved God but that he loved us and sent his Son to be the propitiation for our sins. "*—That big, thick word again, propitiation. Jesus did not only come to bring a sacrifice worthy to God, but he came to BE the sacrifice needed to pay the debt to His Father. And He is the only one that could do that for us.

REVISIT THE TRUTH

Hebrews 1:3-4— *"3 He is the radiance of the glory of God and the exact imprint of his nature, and he upholds the universe by the word of his power. After making purification for sins, he sat down at the right hand of the Majesty on*

> high, **4** *having become as much superior to angels as the name he has inherited is more excellent than theirs."*

Jesus is the "radiance of the glory of God and the exact imprint of his nature." Because He is God, only He was able to take on flesh, make purification for sins, and be raised from the grave by His own power and then seated at the right hand of God the Father. There are cults and false religions that teach Jesus or some humans became gods by the way they lived. People want to believe it is possible to reach a god-like status. That is a lie from the pit of hell.

Jesus took on flesh and lived among us (John 1:1, 14), lived perfectly and died according to the Word. He defeated death by resurrection and remains alive. Jesus's death was necessary for us to have life. Jesus came to bring life to the world.

> Galatians 3:13—*Christ redeemed us from the curse of the law by becoming a curse for us—for it is written, "Cursed is everyone who is hanged on a tree"*

Christ "redeemed us from the curse of the law by *becoming* a curse for us." His death was not a normal death of a man. His death was specifically in place of each child of God. He didn't start sinning but rather became the sin to defeat death. This death was a complete payment for sin to appease the wrath of God and redeem us.

DID JESUS WEAR UNDIES?

PARENT TERMS

My oldest was around 5 years old when she asked this question. After some discussion about Jesus walking with his disciples and teaching them, living life with them and doing normal things, she asked this deep question. And yes, it is a deep question.

The simple answer takes us to "Yes, in a way. He wore undies but not like ours today." We don't get to see many scriptures that describe what Jesus wore or even looked like. We do see that he wore sandals (Matthew 3:11, Mark 1:7, 6:9). He also wore a traditional robe with his prayer garment which had tassels (Mark 6:56). More than likely, He didn't wear extravagant colors because that would cost more money and that would have made Him look more like the Pharisees than He probably wanted to be.

In John 13, we get to see Jesus "remove his outer garments to wash the disciples' feet. Again, Jesus wore undies. He just wore time-appropriate undies without cartoons on them.

One thing we need to remember about questions like this is that the questions have layers even if the child doesn't understand the layers to the question.

So why is it even important to answer the question of whether or not Jesus wore undies? It's important because it points us to the humanity of Christ. One of the most important things to understand about Jesus is that He is 100% man and 100% God. It might seem like a tall task to dive into a discussion on the Incarnation, and it is. But it's not impossible!

Here's the "hurt your head kind of thing" to process through so you can break it down for the kids. Through sin, mankind became completely corrupted. And mere repentance by man for sin could not restore the broken relationship between mankind and God. In order for God to restore the relationship He had with mankind, there needed to be a payment for the sin of like kind. God is not only a loving God, but He is also a just God and could not simply "forgive" the sin as though it never happened. There has to be payment for the sin because God's justice would not allow for sin to go unpunished. He also desired for mankind to be in His presence again and abolishing sin was the only way to make that happen. Therefore, a perfect sacrifice was needed: Jesus.

Jesus, being God and immortal, takes on a human body in a spotless, virgin womb and steps into the world in a different way to become the "second Adam" and make a way for God and mankind to have a redeemed relationship by way of Jesus's perfect sacrificial death and resurrection (Romans 5:12-21, 1 Corinthians 15:44-49).

Jesus has to take on human form in order for there to be a sacrifice of like-kind for the restoration of God to man. John 1 reminds us that the Word became flesh and dwelt among us. He left his perfect seat in Heaven and took on human form to live a perfect life to die for mankind. He did all this while still fully God (Colossians 1:19).

All that to say, yes, Jesus wore undies, and it is important that we know that, because He became a man and died and rose from the grave by His own power for us!

KID TERMS

That is a great question! It's always fun to think about what people used to wear and fun things they did a long, long time ago! We know some of the things that Jesus wore on earth from a couple of different passages like Matthew 3 or Mark 6. We even see him remove the "outer layers" to wash his disciples' feet! So that shows us he had "under layers" so, YES, He wore undies. But not undies like you know it with characters or colors. It was just a simple thing that wrapped around his waist.

You want to know something awesome about the fact that Jesus wore undies? It shows us that Jesus was a man and lived like other people! But we also know that he was God. That means we get to worship a God that is all God and all man! He dressed like other men, felt pain, ate food, walked around and probably smelled a little gross after a long day.

And he became that man for us! He took on a body because He did not have on in Heaven and lived a perfect life and died in that body and rose from the grave! He did that so we could have a relationship with God!

WHY IT'S TRUE

> Galatians 3:13— *"Christ redeemed us from the curse of the law by becoming a curse for us—for it is written, "Cursed is everyone who is hanged on a tree"*

This tells us that Christ redeems us from the curse of the law by becoming the curse for us. He becomes the curse on the cross by becoming a man that could physically die and take upon himself the wrath of God that was due to mankind because of sin.

> Romans 5:12-21— *12 "Therefore, just as sin came into the world through one man, and death through sin, and so death spread to all men because all sinned—13 for sin indeed was in the world before the law was given, but sin is not counted where*

there is no law. *14 Yet death reigned from Adam to Moses, even over those whose sinning was not like the transgression of Adam, who was a type of the one who was to come.*

15 But the free gift is not like the trespass. For if many died through one man's trespass, much more have the grace of God and the free gift by the grace of that one man Jesus Christ abounded for many. 16 And the free gift is not like the result of that one man's sin. For the judgment following one trespass brought condemnation, but the free gift following many trespasses brought justification. 17 For if, because of one man's trespass, death reigned through that one man, much more will those who receive the abundance of grace and the free gift of righteousness reign in life through the one man Jesus Christ.

18 Therefore, as one trespass led to condemnation for all men, so one act of righteousness leads to justification and life for all men. 19 For as by the one man's disobedience the many were made sinners, so by the one man's obedience the many will be made righteous. 20 Now the law came in to increase the trespass, but where sin increased, grace abounded all the more, 21 so that, as sin reigned in death, grace also

> *might reign through righteousness leading to eternal life through Jesus Christ our Lord."*

Paul gives us the truth of Jesus being the second Adam who is able to redeem and give life to all that believe in contrast to the death brought by the first Adam. This is why it's so important to understand that Jesus wasn't only God walking on the Earth. He was fully God and fully Man with a purpose to be the only sacrifice acceptable to God the Father for the payment due because of sin.

REVISIT THE TRUTH

If we jump into 1 Corinthians 15:44-49 we can see more of the "why" for the importance of Jesus becoming a man.

> *"44 It is sown a natural body; it is raised a spiritual body. If there is a natural body, there is also a spiritual body. 45 Thus it is written, "The first man Adam became a living being", the last Adam became a life-giving spirit. 46 But it is not the spiritual that is first but the natural, and then the spiritual. 47 The first man was from the earth, a man of dust; the second man is from heaven. 48 As was the man of dust, so also are those who are of the*

> dust, and as is the man of heaven, so also
> are those who are of heaven. 49 Just as
> we have borne the image of the man of
> dust, we shall also bear the image of the
> man of heaven."

This passage teaches us that the first Adam gave physical life to us, but the second Adam has a life-giving spirit. It's also important to understand that Jesus was not born a man like anyone else. He chose a virgin to form Himself in (untainted by sex) and took on the form of man. The virginity of Mary is important because the sin of man is passed through generations by way of the man's seed. He was not a man that reached a "God-status." John 1:1 tells us, *"In the beginning was the Word, and the Word was with God, and the Word was God."* John 1:14 reminds us that the same Word (Christ) came and tabernacled, or dwelt, among us. The Incarnation of Christ is not something to dismiss or undervalue. Jesus's presence in Heaven prior to creation and His presence on Earth in human form are two truths that make it possible for His sacrifice to be worthy of covering the sins of mankind. Who He is (God the Son) and how He functioned on Earth (God-man) is one of the major differences in the Christian faith compared to other world religions. No other religion believes in a personal, sacrificial God that would humble Himself for the sake of His people.

WHY DID GOD CREATE SATAN IF GOD KNEW SATAN WAS GOING TO DO ALL THE BAD STUFF?

PARENT TERMS

WOW! They busted out the big guns for this one! This question is very deep, and I will provide some other resources for you to dive into for your own understanding. There are a ton of questions like this that could lead us to an answer like "I don't know." Just remember that "I don't know" is acceptable, but I would say it needs to be followed by, "Let's find out together."

It is hard to say the words "I don't know," especially to a child that believes you know everything. There is a hesitation that often comes out of fear, shame, or pride that could keep us from walking through an awesome learning moment for us and for the child. This could encourage your child to know that they don't have to have all the

24

answers to be a Christian and that they can be ok with simply trusting God's plans and interactions without full understanding.

We need to remember that Satan was created by God (Romans 11:36), and he was created good like all creation. The rebellion came from within Satan and not from God because we know there is no darkness found in God (1 John 1:5), and his desire to be exalted like he saw God being praised and worshiped came from his desire to experience the same.

Deuteronomy 6 reminds Israel that they are called to fear the Lord God. They will serve him and by his name alone they will swear allegiance. Satan obviously did not want to fear the Lord nor swear allegiance only to God. He wanted allegiance for himself. We see that Satan and other angels rebelled and God cast them out (Jude 6, 2 Peter 2:4). There are some unknowns in the midst of why God created angels in such a way that they aren't "redeemable" beings, but we do know that they are different from humans. The major difference is that mankind is made in the image of God while angels were created as beings to worship and serve God.

Faith is the next thing we need to chew on for a bit. This question leads to the question, "If God knows everything then He knew man would sin. So why create us if he knew?" In God's economy (how he functions and disperses Himself to humanity), the way he chose to create and allow Satan and mankind to both sin and rebel against our purpose of worshiping and glorifying God would bring Him the most glory ultimately. Is that something we fully grasp? I know I don't. Is it something we can trust because God is all-knowing and good? I believe so.

Faith is trusting that God's plan from beginning to end will bring Him glory. It is trusting in the midst of what we experience in a broken world. You can go down the "matrix hole" all you want about "what ifs." In the end, we can trust that the All-Knowing, All-Powerful, Omnipresent God saw sin and rebellion coming from Satan and allowed it in order that His plan would come to pass.

KID TERMS

That is definitely a question that has been asked for a very long time! Great question! I think one thing we need to talk about is that God knows more than us. In fact, He knows everything. Because he knows everything that has happened and that will happen, we can trust that how he planned things to happen on earth and in heaven is the way that best glorifies Him, and it fits His plan. We might not know the exact answer to something like this, but we trust that God knows. That is called faith.

If we were lost in the woods, it would be hard to hike out if we didn't have a map or if we couldn't see some point of reference to hike towards. The same is true for when we talk about God's plan and how he works on earth. We can get a little better idea of what is going on when we have God's map (the Bible) and when God gives us some points of reference or something to look at and walk towards. In this case, we know that God created everything including Satan. We also know that he was good and decided to rebel against God. God knows everything so it wasn't a surprise to him when Satan rebelled. God allowing Satan to rebel is like the choice God gives us to rebel against His word. He knows that it is coming and he allows it. We only know that by allowing us to make that choice, God also allows the opposite of rebellion in obedience. So, Satan was obedient up until his rebellion.

God used that rebellion to bring his wrath or punishment.

We don't totally get it, but God is able to use bad people or angels and the bad things they do to bring Himself glory in the end. It's hard to think that God punishing someone would bring Him glory, but it is something that shows His power and His justice. And it's hard to think that God wouldn't just stop bad choices, but we can have faith that it will work out and He's in control.

WHY IT'S TRUE

Genesis 1—We trust that God created all things and did so with a plan.

1 Timothy 4:4— *"For everything created by God is good, and nothing is to be rejected if it is received with thanksgiving,"* Everything created, including Satan, was created good. Sin corrupted creation.

Job 1:9-12— ***9** Then Satan answered the Lord and said, "Does Job fear God for no reason? **10** Have you not put a hedge around him and his house and all that he has, on every side? You have blessed the work of his hands, and his possessions have increased in the land. **11** But stretch out your hand and touch all that he has, and he will curse you to your face." **12** And the Lord said to Satan, "Behold, all that he has is in your hand. Only against him do not stretch out your hand." So Satan went out from the presence of the Lord."*

Angels go before God and Satan is among them. He asks permission to interact with Job to test his faithfulness to God. God allows Satan to do so but Satan is always under the control and limitations set by God.

REVISIT THE TRUTH

As believers, we have power over Satan and his schemes.

In Luke 10:17-20—**17** The seventy-two returned with joy, saying, "Lord, even the demons are subject to us in your name!" **18** And he said to them, "I saw Satan fall like lightning from heaven. **19** Behold, I have given you authority to tread on serpents and scorpions, and over all the power of the enemy, and nothing shall hurt you. **20** Nevertheless, do not rejoice in this, that the spirits are subject to you, but rejoice that your names are written in heaven."

The disciples come back rejoicing that even demons were subject to them in their work. Jesus reminds them that He has given them all authority and power over the enemy, and he promises that they cannot be hurt. A special note to make in this passage is that Jesus isn't speaking to physical pain and hurt. But rather, the enemy has no spiritual or lasting power over them any longer. Jesus also reminds them to rejoice in the fact that God knows them and not just that demons listen to them.

We can also rejoice in the fact that Satan and the enemy aren't just defeated in the past with Jesus and the disciples. He is defeated forever and we see John's testimony of what is to come in Revelation 12:7-12. The devil and his angles are cast down forever and the battle is won. We get to respond to the temptations of Satan on the side of victory. We know we have already won!

WHY DO YOU SAY "HOLY" WHEN WE SAY, "IN YOUR HOLY NAME WE PRAY"?

PARENT TERMS

Kids pay attention to little details more than we realize. One of the most humbling things to learn as a parent or an adult around children frequently is the specific phrases you speak often. I've heard it said that if you record yourself in a conversation, you can hear your frequent phrases. Well, I didn't need to record myself. I just have kids that hear everything! In this case, I am perfectly fine with my kids hearing me and repeating this phrase.

We started something new when this question came about. We called it "copy pray." I would say a phrase and the girls would copy it. After a couple of weeks of this, A asked this simple question and I was so glad that she did.

A simple thing we can teach our kids is that God is holy. As adults, I think we just assume that people know that and get it. But our kids need to hear truths about who God is and why He is different from the other gods our kids will hear about.

God is holy. Leviticus 11:44 tells us "For I am the Lord your God. Consecrate yourselves therefore, and be holy, for I am holy. You shall not defile yourselves with any swarming thing that crawls on the ground." 1 Peter 1:16 reminds us that we are called to be holy like him. This holiness is an "apartness" or sacredness about God. Everything about God is different from who we are. This can be confusing because man was made in His image. But the image we are created in is not the same as the essence of God.

Pictures will almost always disappoint. Think about when you are shopping for a home, the pictures look beautiful online but when you pull up to the house, reality tells a different story. A picture of something so magnificent as the Grand Canyon could even be worth hanging on your wall. But that picture pales in comparison to standing on the edge of the canyon and gazing across at God's beautiful creation. No picture could really do it justice; we are the picture of who God is and we reflect his beauty. But no matter how special and beautiful, placed beside the real thing, His true holiness puts even those whom he made holy to shame. Our best, as scripture tells us, is but "filthy rags" compared to the reality of our God and his holiness.

His holiness describes the truth of who God is; He is apart. And this is something we need to remind ourselves daily. One, we need to remember that God is holy to view God properly. Two, we should be reminded of His holiness because we, as followers of Christ, are called to be holy, sacred and set apart, like Christ.

Using biblical terms to speak of who God is, using different names of God, and describing who God is according to His Word helps us and our children know God more. It is an easy step in discipleship with our kids.

KID TERMS

I want you to know certain things about God and who He is. When we say His name is holy, we mean it's different from any other name. There have been other people named Jesus in this world, but the name of God that we see in the Bible is a special, separate name. The word "Holy" means something like this: if you have something that is so special and there isn't anything like it in the world and there never will be, you will probably set it to the side to display it. That is a little bit like what we are doing when we say, "your holy name." We are giving His name honor and respect to say that He is God and we are not. It helps us remember that we are not God and that God is good and different from any other god we might hear about in life.

WHY IT'S TRUE

The Psalmist repeatedly speaks of God as holy. Psalms 99 and 111 are good examples

Major and minor prophets—Isa, Hosea

> Isaiah 6:2-3—"*2 Above him stood the seraphim. Each had six wings: with two he covered his face, and with two he covered his feet, and with two he flew. 3 And one called to another and said:*
>
> "*Holy, holy, holy is the Lord of hosts; the whole earth is full of his glory!*"

The vision of Isaiah shows us the power and majesty in the holiness of God. We see a glimpse of Heaven and how there are angels singing of God's holiness for eternity. In fact, His holiness is so great that the angels before Him cannot even look upon Him and they covered their feet.

As John describes what he sees in Heaven in the book of Revelation, one major theme is the repetition of declaring God Holy by the angels he created.

> Revelation 4:8—"*And the four living creatures, each of them with six wings, are full of eyes all around and within, and day and night they never cease to say, "Holy, holy, holy, is the Lord God Almighty, who was and is and is to come!*"

> Proverbs 22:6—*"Train up a child in the way he should go; even when he is old he will not depart from it."*

We are called as parents to teach our children the Truth of God's Word. Repeating characteristics of God and talking about His love often will play a huge part in the discipleship of a child.

REVISIT THE TRUTH

> Revelation 4:8—*"And the four living creatures, each of them with six wings, are full of eyes all around and within, and day and night they never cease to say, "Holy, holy, holy, is the Lord God Almighty, who was and is and is to come!"*

There is a reason that God's creation cries out the truth of His holiness. That reason is because it's true. John gives us a picture of what God allowed him to see in the book of Revelation. There are four living creatures that were created by God, and they fly before Him at His throne and declare, "Holy, holy, holy, is the Lord God Almighty, who was and is and is to come." Their sole purpose is to glorify God by declaring His holiness in Heaven. Think about that for a second. Those creatures aren't standing out in front of a crowd of people that don't know God and need to hear the Gospel. They are before the God

DID JESUS WEAR UNDIES?

Almighty with no other witnesses simply praising the God of creation for who He is.

That picture of heaven, that small glimpse, is a driving force as to why we should continuously declare God holy. That is the truth that reminds us that we are who we are and that God is God. He is a just, good, righteous, and holy God. We are redeemed saints that are being made new in him.

GOD + ME—
Gods interactions with me in life and salvation

HOW DID GOD MAKE US?

PARENT TERMS

Words spoken from God can be powerful and life changing. The words I speak to my wife, to my children, and to my family come with a weight or power behind them. This power is only in existence because of the relationship I have with each person, and that relationship will determine how specific words can or will be interpreted. If I say "no" to my child, it has a different weight to it than when I say "no" to my parents. That "no" has even more power when it comes from God. That power comes from the relationship status of who God is. When my kids hear me say it, I have an authority over them that has been established since birth. When my parents hear it from me and the realization that they have had the power position over me from earlier in my life, it's heard differently. When God says it, we interpret it differently because of his position. And his position is ALL POWERFUL. His position is ALL KNOWING. His position is CREATOR. Since he is all powerful, all knowing, and Creator, when I respond to this question with the answer "He SPOKE us into being" the theological basis of God's POWER must be addressed.

We can't fully comprehend the depth of speaking things into existence. I understand creating things from elements or parts that exist already. From God's perspective, it was only Him (existing as Father/Son/Spirit) in the beginning. He didn't stumble upon a vacant planet and happen to figure out how to create things. He chose to speak as his creative choice of action. The idea that God chose to speak instead of simply create always reminds me that words are important. God's words are important as well as ours but only because our ability to speak comes from God.

God existed and then spoke all things (known and unknown to us today) into existence. From the Earth, he made mankind by breathing the spirit of life into mankind and creating mankind to be image bearers of God. That was unique compared to the rest of creation and God's response was that it was "very good."

God didn't create out of magic or left-over parts of something. He created all things out of nothing. As we grow in our understanding of who God is and His power, His might, His love, we will continue to believe in faith that God created all things *ex nihilo* (out of nothing).

KID TERMS

We have an awesome relationship with God because of how He chose to create humans. You see, when it was just God, He decided to create everything! And He is so powerful that He just said it, and it happened! It wasn't magic or a spell. It was simply His words that made everything we see happen. When we look in the Bible, we see how he made different things each day for 6 days. Then on the 6th day, He made humans. He took some dirt that he created and formed Adam, and then He breathed into him, giving him life. And then we see that he had Adam take a nap and he used a rib from Adam to make Eve and breathed that same life into her.

It's sort of hard to understand that he made everything out of nothing because we can only make things out of what we have. But that shows us how much power God has! It's not JUST that He can make anything, but He can simply speak it into existence! Our faith helps us understand this truth and others like it that deal with things we can't see or do ourselves.

WHY IT'S TRUE

> Genesis 1:27, 31—27 *"So God created man in his own image, in the image of God he created him; male and female he created them."*

31a *"And God saw everything that he had made, and behold, it was very good."*

We see the creation story unfold in Genesis 1 and 2. From this we see the detail God took in His creation to breathe life into mankind and make us in His own image (not physically in His image). Genesis 1:1 starts "In the beginning." This gives us the picture of the beginning of what we know of as "time." God then creates the heavens and earth in time and from there the creation unfolds in His sustaining power.

John 8:58— *"Truly, truly, I say to you, before Abraham was, I am."* Jesus even speaks to His prior existence with a statement of claiming "I AM." This is claiming that He is 1) God 2) prior in existence to man 3) All authority. The authority in this name is the power behind creating everything and sustaining it (Col 1:16-18).

2 Timothy 3:16-17— *"All scripture is breathed out by God and profitable for teaching, for reproof, for correction, and for training in righteousness, that the man of God may be complete, equipped for every good work."*—The same powerful voice and breath that spoke all things into existence also spoke the scripture into

existence. Words are the chosen means of communication by God to connect to the world. And we are called to speak those same words to others.

REVISIT THE TRUTH

Kids are curious. And we should invite that curiosity because we are teaching them so many things all the time and they are trying to line it all out in their heads. I have to remind myself that my kids don't know what I know. I think God reminds me of that same truth in regards to what I don't know compared to Him.

This question of **HOW DID GOD MAKE US?** should bring about more questions and thoughts on creation and what it means for God to have created ALL THINGS. Again, our minds can comprehend making something from preexisting elements. But the idea of creating out of nothing truly goes beyond our brains.

> Colossians 1:15-18— *"He is the image of the invisible God, the firstborn of all creation. For by him all things were created, in heaven and on earth, visible and invisible, whether thrones or dominions or rulers or authorities—all things were created through him and for him. And he is before all things, and*

> *in him all things hold together. And he*
> *is the head of the body, the church. He*
> *is the beginning, the firstborn from the*
> *dead, that in everything he might be*
> *preeminent."*

This passage is teaching us that Jesus, The Word, is the image of God. That truth declares to us His authority and power. This is the same power of creation in Genesis. And we see that through Christ, all things have been made. There is nothing on earth or space that was created by anyone or anything else. When we ask HOW things were created, we can't forget to talk about the WHY. Verse 16 tells us that "all things were created through him and for him." Why were we created? We were created for Him! We were created for His Glory! The only being worthy of praise and honor and glory created all things to bring himself more glory and praise. That would be a selfish act if the being wasn't deserving of it all.

CAN GOD HOLD ME WHILE I SLEEP?

PARENT TERMS

This came on a night when A didn't want to sleep because she was afraid of a bad dream. We prayed for rest and good dreams. She wanted one of us to hold her and sleep with her that night. When one of my girls comes to me with the need of being held, I feel a couple of things. One, I am humbled that they are comforted by being in my arms. And two, I am so grateful that they come to me and feel safe in my arms.

When she said, "Daddy, can you just hold me until I fall asleep?" the world stopped. Nothing else mattered to me until she felt safe and peaceful enough to fall asleep. I know I am not the strongest man in the world, but, to her, I'm the strongest Daddy she has.

After the physical need was met, I could then sit with her and explain to her about times that I am afraid and how I trust God to "hold me" and bring me peace with His presence and truth.

We talked about how God is everywhere (omnipresent). We talked about how God can be in Heaven on His throne and near us. He can be walking in the Garden with Adam and Eve, and sustaining existence from Heaven at the same time.

God's presence is real and "thick" in our home. Can he hold us with physical arms? No, because God doesn't actually have a physical body like us (John 4:24), but we talked about what happens and what feelings we have when we are held by Mommy or Daddy (or someone we trust). Peace, love, rest. All these feelings come from the Lord and they come from trusting the "holder". God blesses us with people we can trust to experience those feelings physically while He fills us with peace and rest spiritually and emotionally. Jesus is even called the Prince of Peace in Isaiah 9:6-7 and we are promised this same peace because of WHO Jesus is and the authority He has over this world.

KID TERMS

Even though God the Father doesn't have arms like us to pick us up when we are afraid, He gives trusted people the ability to hold or be near to us to help us feel safe. While we "fill up" with safe feelings and peace when someone holds us, we can remind each other of God being close to us everywhere we go! The great thing is we don't have to even ask Him to be near; He already is because He is everywhere! And if we are scared of something, we can have peace knowing that the Prince of Peace is close to us and has the power to overcome ANY trouble that comes our way! Since God has all the power, we know that He will take care of us.

Just like you feel safe when someone you trust stays close to you because you believe they can keep you safe, when you are afraid we can practice trusting that God is right here with us!

WHY IT'S TRUE

> Ephesians 2:14–17 "**14** For he himself is our peace, who has made us both one and has broken down in his flesh the dividing wall of hostility **15** by abolishing the law of commandments expressed in ordinances, that he might create in himself one new man in place of the two, so making peace, **16** and might reconcile us both to God in one body through the cross, thereby killing the hostility. **17** And he came and preached peace to you who were far off and peace to those who were near."

He is our peace, and he promises to bring us peace, that's why we go to him when we don't have peace about something. When we remind ourselves and our kids that the Creator of peace is with us on a regular basis, that Truth will become what we rest in during times of unrest.

> John 14:27 *"Peace I leave with you; my peace I give to you. Not as the world gives do I give to you. Let not your hearts be troubled, neither let them be afraid."*

We also talked about how the fruit of the Spirit will flow from how we live. Gal 5:22—If the Spirit lives in us, peace will overflow

> John 10:25-29— *"**25** Jesus answered them, "I told you, and you do not believe. The works that I do in my Father's name bear witness about me, **26** but you do not believe because you are not among my sheep. **27** My sheep hear my voice, and I know them, and they follow me. **28** I give them eternal life, and they will never perish, and no one will snatch them out of my hand."*

Jesus is talking about His oneness with the Father and the power that the Father has to save and secure His own children. We are given a promise from Jesus that no one is able to snatch us from the Hand of God. This is emphasized by Paul in Romans 8:38-39 when Paul writes "For I am sure that neither death nor life, nor angels nor rulers, nor things present nor things to come, nor powers nor height nor depth, nor anything else in all creation, will be able to separate us from the love of God in Christ Jesus our Lord."—Once we are being held by God, we are secure!

REVISIT THE TRUTH

> Philippians 4:6-9—This is not a situation that should happen nightly. We want to teach the truth of God's peace to our kids and give them the tools to walk in that truth. Spending time in this passage together as a family is a great start!

> Verses 6-7—*"Do not be anxious about anything but in everything by prayer and supplication(begging) with thanksgiving let your requests be made known to God. And the PEACE of God, which surpasses all understanding, will guard your hearts and your minds in Christ Jesus."*

I added the emphasis on prayer and supplication for a reason. Supplication isn't a word I use often and definitely not with my kids. This passage shows us that we can go to God in prayer and beg for Him to hear our requests and His PEACE will guard our hearts from allowing lies to come in and bring fear.

> Verses 8-9— *"Finally, brothers, whatever is true, whatever is honorable, whatever is just, whatever is pure, whatever is lovely, whatever is commendable, if there is any excellence, if there is anything worthy of praise, think about these things. What you have learned and received and heard and seen in me—practice these things and the God of Peace will* **be with you.** *"*

Paul has lived a great enough example that he tells the church to mimic what they have seen him do. What did he do? He thought about things that are true, honorable, just, pure, lovely, commendable, excellent, and worthy of praise. Thinking on those things and reminding himself of those things that God has provided is how he practically reminded himself of the God of Peace that was with him. That is how we remind ourselves and our kids that the God of Peace is with us.

DO I GET TO GO TO HEAVEN AND SEE POPS?

PARENT TERMS

This can be a tough question because missing a loved one is universal and children often don't have the words to express their feelings. This specific question needs to be answered according to the current spiritual standing of the child. Ultimately, the child is asking if they get to go to Heaven. And that specific truth needs to be addressed based on the child's age and salvation story.

In our situation Pops is my father-in-law. He passed away in 2015 after a battle with cancer. A was only about 1.5yrs old when he died. She does remember him a little and will periodically bring him up in conversation. It's always a blessing when she does because it allows us to relive some of the great memories we have of him. We get to continue to talk about his fun side and wacky behavior. We get to remind our kids of how he loved us and would love them fiercely if he were still here.

More importantly, we have the blessing of sharing the legacy of faith that he cultivated in his children which overflowed into our family and into his grandchildren even after he went home to Heaven. Because of that faith, we try to talk about him often. So, one day, she asked the question, "Do I get to go to Heaven and see Pops?"

The easy, comfortable answer is, "Yes, honey. You will see him again someday." But If I know that there is a possibility of that being false, why would I want to speak that to my daughter? Some might say to just tell her "yes" because she is young enough to forget what you said that day. But something we learned early on about A is that she remembers EVERYTHING we say, like, scary details! So, I didn't want to just pass over this question and not give her the truth. Remember, it's easier to build on truth than tear down lies and hope the foundation doesn't get damaged. (If you missed the intro, this might not make sense.)

What did I tell her? I told her, "I hope so." I hope so because my hope was that she would eventually have a saving relationship with God and that she would be known by Him. I hope that she would see her need for a savior and that Christ is that savior she needs. I hope that she knows God wants to have a relationship with her. I hope she would hear the truth that God loves her and desires to have her be a part of His church.

Then we got to talk about how we can trust that Pops is in Heaven. He knew he was a sinner in need of grace. He surrendered his life to Christ, he repented of his sins, and he declared Jesus as Lord. We can hope and trust that God completed the work He started in his as well as other loved ones that declared Him Lord.

So, when she believes the same Truth of who Jesus is and that she has the same need as a sinner, repents of her sins, she will get to praise Jesus together with Pops and all the other loved ones that went before her.

KID TERMS

Perspective of child that doesn't have a relationship with Christ

The beautiful thing about Heaven is that if we have a relationship with God like Pops, then YES, we get to see and hug Pops in Heaven when Jesus takes us home. Everyone that is a child of God has the blessing of being in Heaven forever with God and those that love him. What's really cool to think about is that we will even be able to love Pops MORE than what we could love him on earth because there isn't sin in Heaven. God's presence will make it possible for us to love each other more and more forever!

*If a child has repented and expressed faith in Christ, lean into this truth of his or her salvation even more. You won't be speaking in hope of understanding, but rather in the hope that God will complete the work He has started in the child.

WHY IT'S TRUE

Romans 3:23—*"for all have sinned and fall short of the glory of God," lets us know that we all sin and we need a savior.*

Romans 6:23— *"For the wages of sin is death, but the free gift of God is eternal life in Christ Jesus our Lord."*

This shows us that because of our sin, we will all die physically and spiritually unless we are saved.

Romans 5:8—*"but God shows his love for us in that while we were still sinners, Christ died for us."*

God has provided the way for us to be saved and have a relationship with Him. He did this before we repented or even knew we needed him to do it.

Romans 10:9-10— *"because, if you confess with your mouth that Jesus is Lord and believe in your heart that God raised him from the dead, you will be saved. For with the heart one believes and is justified, and with the mouth one confesses and is saved."*

We are saved by repentance and confession of our sin, which is our declaration of Jesus as our Savior.

Phil 1:6 "And I am sure of this, that he who began a good work in you will bring it to completion at the day of Jesus Christ."

The work of our salvation is not done by us. It is also not maintained and completed by us. Because of this truth, when we speak with children about the hope of seeing someone they love in Heaven and that loved one is a believer, then we can be confident in saying "yes" because the hope is in God's work in both of them. This first chapter of Philippians shows us Paul's desire to be in Heaven with Jesus. We understand that children (and even adults) will want to see their loved ones again. We don't have to pull them away from that idea but we can also spend time reminding them of the beautiful picture of Jesus waiting for His children to enter the gates and into His arms.

REVISIT THE TRUTH

This is a perfect time to walk through the Roman Road and speak to the need for repentance, the reality of sin, and the power of God's saving grace.

Romans 3:23—All have sinned
Romans 6:23—Because of sin, we all die
Romans 5:8—God made a way out of death, by Christ dying for us
Romans 10:9-10—Confess these truths, believe in who Christ is as your Savior, you will be saved

WHY DIDN'T JESUS CONTROL HER WHEN SHE DREW ON THE WALL? (When we do bad things?)

PARENT TERMS

It's always fun when a child brings up a question related to free will and the battle of two natures. This was a simple, straightforward question asked in the playroom of our home. The girls were having fun coloring and creating some great art when I had to step into the other room. In the few seconds I was gone, one of the girls decided to "create" on the wall. It wasn't the first time and absolutely wasn't the last time someone colored on a wall in our house!

God did not make us robots. He doesn't control our every move like a puppet. He created us as free beings with the purpose to worship Him freely. Forced obedience is not true obedience. Obedience to God should be out of love, reverence and awe of who God is and the fact that only God deserves to be praised and honored.

Genesis 3 shows us Adam and Eve decided to disobey God. They were instructed by God to not eat from a specific tree. But they listened to the half-truths and lies from Satan and decided to trust what he said over what God told them. They weren't given a long list of "don'ts." They were shown an entire, full garden and invited to eat it. They were told of the danger in eating from one single tree. They were told that it would change the way they live forever because death would come from it.

God was trying to protect them from being separated from him. Up until that point when sin entered the picture, Adam and Eve were able to have a very close relationship with God, so close that they walked with Him in the garden. They had uninterrupted communication and time with God in His presence.

He gave mankind the ability to think and choose. Unfortunately, our choices, apart from the grace of God, will lead to sin. Adam and Eve's choice brought sin into the lineage of man passed down from human men (important to note when discussing the virgin birth).

This sin leads to death and a broken spirit that will always choose sin and oneself over glorifying God. God created us to follow him. After sin entered the garden, all people have sinned (Romans 3:23). That means before our lives are given to God, we will choose to follow what we want to do, and God will allow us to do that. We do not want to do what God wants to do until the Spirit of God lives in us and changes our hearts. There are only two masters to choose from in this world and our sinful spirits will choose the enemy of God.

After God redeems us we will live life fighting against those desires to choose what we want and what God wants for us. It tells us in Romans 7:14–25 that this is a constant battle and will continue until we are called home to Heaven or Jesus returns.

KID TERMS

Do you always obey your parents? No. That is because you want to do what you want to do. You know and trust that your parents love you and want the best for you, but you have something inside of you that tells you to do your own thing. When we lose focus on that trust, that is our flesh or our sin nature. We all have it and it's the broken part of us that Jesus came to fix by dying on the cross.

God doesn't want us to be robots and not be able to choose to love or obey Him. He wants us to choose His way over what we want. He knows the best way for that to happen is to save us from our sinful minds and hearts and give us a new life and way to see things. This new nature or life will help us to want to love and obey him.

WHY IT'S TRUE

Romans 7-8—The sin nature will constantly fight against the Spirit's movement in our hearts. The desires of the flesh run deep in us and it takes a lifetime to practice disciplines to rid our daily lives of allowing that temptation to sit at the door and give birth to sin. The "control" that we would want from God so we could stop sinning doesn't happen like a magic trick. As believers, we do live on the side of victory and we know that we are redeemed and made new. We have to constantly remind ourselves and submit to a mindful renewal and refining throughout our lives (sanctification).

Romans 3:23—All of us have sinned and we will continue to sin. We fall short of the perfect standard of God. That includes everyone born of man. We are not able to escape sin in this world. Our only hope is to place our faith in Christ to be redeemed by Him.

REVISIT THE TRUTH

Genesis 1—This is a tough passage to look at and not scream. We want to tell Adam and Eve that what they were told by God was the truth! It's hard to believe that they listened to the lies of Satan and didn't rest in the truth that God was protecting them. They were told that God was trying to keep them from becoming like him. They believed they were being held back. That is what I see often in my kids. It seems like I tell them to not do something or to stop doing something and they think I'm just trying to kill the fun.

> Psalm 51:10—*"Create in me a clean heart, O God, and renew a right spirit within me."*
> This should be a constant prayer over us and over our children. Our minds a linked to the habitual nature of sin and we need our minds to be renewed daily. This will help us in walking through sanctification and moving away from sinful behaviors and desires.

In reality I am trying to protect them from physical harm, emotional harm or spiritual harm. But, their flesh wants what it wants and if they don't look at the consequences, they will repeat the same sin over and over again (much like we do) because we don't learn. Our flesh can even lie to us and tell us that we can do the exact same thing but get a completely different outcome.

WHY DID JUDAS WANT TO GO WITH JESUS IF HE WAS GOING TO BE MEAN?

PARENT TERMS

As kids learn more about God and his power, questions like this are going to come up. Also, as the topic of sin continues to solidify in their minds, they will begin to question the actions of others as well as their own actions.

This question points us to a few things we know about God and about mankind. One thing we can know is that Jesus did know that Judas was going to betray him because Jesus is God. That means that Jesus chose Judas to follow him even though He knew what would happen. One very important thing this teaches us about mankind is that we are all sinners. All of us have a sinful nature and we want to satisfy our flesh.

While looking at Judas and his life, we don't know of any other instances that something like this happened or was even considered by him or any other disciple. We only see glimpses of this process. The idea that Judas started following Jesus with betraying him as an end goal is not backed by scripture.

Luke 22:3-6 and John 13:21-30 give us the clearest picture of how things shifted in Judas to give him the desire to betray the Rabbi that cared for him, taught him, and walked with him for years. These passages reference "Satan entered into him." So, we see Judas allowing the enemy to enter him and direct his decisions. We don't know when the first thought of betrayal occurred in Judas. We do see this final decision to betray after Jesus dips the bread and offers it to Judas. This offering of the bread (now seen as the body of Christ) is believed by some scholars to be the final offer of love to Judas by Jesus. This offering was then taken by Judas and fueled an evil decision by his flesh to allow Satan to enter him.

His original intent probably wasn't to travel with Jesus for a few years and betray him. Judas handled the money and at some point was probably approached with opportunities to give up Jesus to authorities. Unfortunately, his flesh allowed the temptation to give birth to sin and he finally betrayed Jesus.

KID TERMS

We know Judas was just like all of us. He was a sinner that needed a savior. He probably didn't start following Jesus to eventually betray him. Judas was a money guy and it's believed that he handled whatever money the group had while traveling. We can take a guess on why he even thought about betraying Jesus. One idea could be that he was frustrated that this famous guy he was following wasn't someone that seemed to be into making money off that fame. In fact, it was the opposite.

We actually see in a couple of verses that Judas gave control to Satan when he went to make a deal with the Jewish leaders to betray Jesus. Again, we don't see anything about Judas acting like this before the Last Supper when Jesus even tells Judas and the other disciples that he would be betrayed by one of them. He was probably a faithful follower up until this point. In fact, it looks like from the verses about the Last supper that Judas was sitting close to Jesus which is a seat of honor.

It looks like there was probably a temptation for Judas before this happened and it grew to sin and he finally gave in to that sin. He knew where to go and what to do so the men he spoke to probably already talked to him about a plan. Satan did not just take over his body and make him do it. Satan can't do that to people. This was something that Judas invited in and he made the decision to do.

WHY IT'S TRUE

> Luke 22:3-6— *"Then Satan entered Judas, called Iscariot, one of the Twelve. 4 And Judas went to the chief priests and the officers of the temple guard and*

> *discussed with them how he might betray*
> *Jesus. 5 They were delighted and agreed*
> *to give him money. 6 He consented, and*
> *watched for an opportunity to hand Jesus*
> *over to them when no crowd was present."*

Judas was not a perfect person and we know the enemy will try and convince us that following him is best for us. Judas was in charge of money and we see him seeking this opportunity for money. Sadly, when money is involved we can be like Judas and ignore what we are doing in sin or even justify for any reason. Judas could have thought that Jesus would be able to escape. And I don't believe Judas would have known that the beating and crucifixion was going to happen after he betrayed Jesus. That is another way the enemy blinds us from understanding and seeing what consequences could come from our choices.

> John 13:21-30— *"21 After saying*
> *these things, Jesus was troubled in his*
> *spirit, and testified, "Truly, truly, I say to*
> *you, one of you will betray me." 22 The*
> *disciples looked at one another, uncertain*
> *of whom he spoke. 23 One of his*
> *disciples, whom Jesus loved, was reclining*
> *at table at Jesus' side, 24 so Simon Peter*
> *motioned to him to ask Jesus of whom he*
> *was speaking. 25 So that disciple, leaning*
> *back against Jesus, said to him, "Lord,*

who is it?" 26 Jesus answered, "It is he to whom I will give this morsel of bread when I have dipped it." When he had dipped the morsel, he gave it to Judas, the son of Simon Iscariot. 27 Then after he had taken the morsel, Satan entered into him. Jesus said to him, "What you are going to do, do quickly." 28 Now no one at the table knew why he said this to him. 29 Some thought that, because Judas had the moneybag, Jesus was telling him, "Buy what we need for the feast," or that he should give something to the poor. 30 So, after receiving the morsel of bread, he immediately went out. And it was night."

Jesus knew He was going to be betrayed. He even spends time telling His disciples that one of them was going to do it soon. The beautiful thing about Jesus knowing He was about to be betrayed by someone that had spent the last few years with Him is that He was still sitting with him at the table. He didn't kick him out. He even gave him instruction to go do what his heart wanted to do. This of course fulfilled prophecy and Judas might not have known exactly what was to come of it. And we don't know if this was the first time Judas thought about this. It seems like from this passage and Luke 22 that Judas knew who to go to in order that he would get paid to betray Jesus. So, it is not inconceivable to think that Judas or others had been offered something prior to this time.

REVISIT THE TRUTH

A very important aspect of the situation with Judas is that we need to remember we are sinners just like him. Romans 3:23 reminds us that we have all sinned and fall short of the glory of God. That means if we allow sin to just sit at our door, we could let it in and allow it to give birth and into sin we fall. Judas sought out the leaders to betray Jesus. Almost in the same breath, Jesus explains to Peter how he will soon deny Jesus 3 times. Denial is different from an open betrayal, but it is still sin and falling short of the glory of God. Judas was possessed while Peter was not. Judas made his choice for personal gain while Peter chose to protect himself.

Judas sought out the sin while Peter was not prepared. It is important to note that Judas did not have the indwelling Holy Spirit because no one did. So, possession was possible. This is not something possible for a believer because no spirit can remove the Holy Spirit from a believer. It is something invited in.

WHY DOES GOD LOVE OUR SOULS?

PARENT TERMS

It's not every day that we get to talk about the *imago dei*. Mankind is created in the image of God. That is what separates us from the rest of creation. No other thing that God created had the breath of life breathed into it. That special thing is what sets us apart from the rest of the world. Our souls (spirits) are the unique aspects that differentiate us from a dog or cow or a whale. We were given bodies and minds but also a soul that is an eternal element of who we are.

Our bodies and our minds will fade and die. Our souls will live forever. Our soul is redeemable by God. Our minds are constantly needing to be renewed because of our sinful nature. Our souls are redeemed and secured by the blood of Christ. Our bodies slowly decay and will eventually die and rot. Our souls are given eternal security in Christ's death and will be placed in new, heavenly bodies.

Our souls make us different. God even declares us "Very good" at the time of creation. God didn't send His Son to die on a cross to redeem a dog. He sent his Son to live a perfect life, die, resurrect, and live so that our souls could live for eternity with him in the new Heaven. The soul makes us different from the rest of creation. This is a major element linked to the Image of God that we are made in. God is triune and we have made us in an image of this with mind/body/soul.

KID TERMS

We are God's special creation. God created everything and he said it was good. Then he created humans and gave us souls. The Bible said He breathed life into us. This is what makes us different from animals or other living things. We are made in the image of God. That means we have a soul, also known as our spirit, that will live forever. The soul, or spirit, is the part of us that is redeemed or bought back by God when we become followers of Christ. That's something other living things don't have. We have bodies and minds that will eventually be gone forever. But God gave us a soul that will live forever. That's the part of us that he wants to save. Our mind and body are going to die because of sin but God will give us a new body in Heaven!

WHY IT'S TRUE

> Genesis 5:1—*"This is the book of the generations of Adam. When God created man, he made him in the likeness of God."*

God created all things perfectly. The design of mankind was in the image of God. Mankind broke that image with sin. The foundation of who we are as humans is in the image of God and we are called to live and above the God that formed us in His image. After sin, only God can restore us to the image of our creator. That is what Paul explains in Ephesians 4 and Colossians 3.

> Ephesians 4:24—*"and to put on the new self, created after the likeness of God in true righteousness and holiness."*

> Colossians 3:10—*"and have put on the new self, which is being renewed in knowledge after the image of its creator."*

Believers are given instruction to remove the sinful behaviors in their lives so they can reflect the true image of their creator. Sin in our lives covers and denies the holy image we were created in and God desires to make us back into that image.

REVISIT THE TRUTH

The best picture of how we are made in the image of God is the fact that we are made in body, mind, and spirit. God is triune (Father, Son and Spirit) and we reflect that 3 in 1 aspect in how we are made. There are three elements that make up one person. But we wouldn't say that the body, spirit or mind are each a person. The idea of separate persons helps us understand how the three persons of our triune God can function as 3 in 1 and still be only one God.

Of course, the analogy fails as you dissect it more and more. Nothing truly gives us a perfectly clear picture of the Trinity because it is an idea that explains an infinite God. Our body and mind will eventually fade and die. Our spirit/soul is eternal. God created us to remain after our physical bodies die. Our spirits will remain either in His Holy presence in Heaven or they will remain eternally in Hell with the wrath of God pouring over them. His love for our souls/spirit is shown in this truth. He desires for all to be saved and remain eternally in his presence.

Romans 8:16 and Ephesians 2:10 speak to the truth that we are His children. We are declared as set apart and different from the world. It reminds me of the book *You are Special*. The characters have to be reminded throughout the story that they are special because they are made by the creator and their value does not come from what others say about them. We need to remember this same truth about our value and our Creator. We are special and unique because of who our Creator is.

WHY DO YOU READ YOUR BIBLE EVERY MORNING?

PARENT TERMS

One of the biggest lessons I've learned as a parent is that my kids watch me. They see me do things in a routine that I don't even think about doing anymore. The tricky part about that is that they see the good and the bad things. I'm beyond thankful that my kids saw this good thing. Are we perfect in our rhythms? Not exactly. I think it's a good thing that kids see us in our imperfections as well. This will help in scenarios like this to teach them that progress and consistency are the target, not perfection in a legalistic way. I know we are called to be perfect as our Heavenly Father is perfect (Matthew 5:48) but that is for another discussion.

So why do we read our Bible every day? To answer that, we start with talking about what the Bible is. The Bible is the active, living Word of God. It tells the story of God's creation of man, mankind's walk to and away from God, God's redemption story of His creation and the salvation of His church. The Bible is one way God communicates to us about who He is and how He has interacted with people and how He will return. The Bible gives us clarity about our need for God, our Savior. It speaks to us so that we are able to teach, rebuke, correct, and love according to how God desires for us. It prepares us for questions like these. It comforts us in our struggles and enables us to speak truth over others in their times of need.

Paul writes in his letter to Timothy, 2 Timothy 4:2, to preach the word and be prepared "in season and out of season." I think we are called to actively seek the truth and absorb it so that we can speak it to ourselves and others whenever needed.

I was in college having lunch with two guys that I went to high school with and one was a believer and the other an atheist. We were talking about God and the idea of "why do you believe." During the discussion, I reached into my bag to grab my Bible. My atheist friend grabbed my Bible and threw it across the room and said, "I don't want you to read me something; I want to hear what you know and believe!" That interaction pushed me to want to KNOW the Word.

Another reason why we should read the Word constantly is that it feeds us. It is the LIVING Word. It brings life through the spoken Word of God. It is our nourishment. We need the Word like we need food. Our souls can become "malnourished" just like our physical bodies if we don't care for them.

The concept of abiding in Christ is a major reason why a follower of Christ should be in the Word. John 15, Christ talks about his followers being branches connected to the true vine. The vine gives life to the branches. There wouldn't be branches without the vine. If the vine dies, the branch dies. We get to be a branch connected and abiding in the vine of life. Being connected to the vine is what brings us life!

KID TERMS

When you wake up in the morning, what is one of the first things (after going potty) that you want to do? Eat! After sleeping 8+ hours and not drinking water, our bodies need to be fed. And that feeling of being hungry isn't something that you have to teach your body. Your body just knows you need it. You do learn over time what the feeling means. But when you are a baby and you are hungry, you just cry. So, an adult needs to learn what that cry means. Sometimes your body tells you by a little cramp in your stomach. Sometimes it literally talks to you and you hear your stomach "growl." So, understanding the growl is learned.

That is the same thing for our spiritual bodies. Our souls growl for God and time with Him. Our souls are made to know we need God, but we need to be taught what that growl in our soul means. How we do that is by spending consistent time in

God's Word. We learn how God spoke to people. We learn His truths about who He is and what He wants for us in a relationship with Him. We learn this from the Bible. And as we learn those truths, we can share them with other people and encourage them to read the Word and learn the same things and know those truths in their hearts!

WHY IT'S TRUE

We see throughout the Psalms that mankind has a yearning and a thirst for God and His Word (Psalms 24:6, 27:8, 42:1-4, 63:1, 73:26). These passages also speak to the need for God and his word to feed and keep man alive.

> Psalm 42:1-4—*"As a deer pants for flowing streams, so pants my soul for you, O God. My soul thirsts for God, for the living God. When shall I come and appear before God? My tears have been my food day and night, while they say to me all the day long, "Where is your God?" These things I remember, as I pour out my soul: how I would go with the throng and lead them in procession to the house of God with glad shouts and songs of praise, a multitude keeping festival."*

Our soul knows it needs the Lord. Being made in the image of God, we have in our beings the desire, the need, the passion for God. Unfortunately, if we aren't taught what that "growl" is and how to fulfill that desire, we will fill that void with other perishing things.

> 2 Timothy 3:16-17—*"All Scripture is breathed out by God and profitable for teaching, for reproof, for correction, and for training in righteousness, that the man of God may be complete, equipped for every good work."*

We get to have the Word of God as a tool and refiner in our lives. We start by reading it and knowing it so it will be used in our spirits by the power of the Holy Spirit to change us, teach us, correct us so that we may be complete and equipped for every good work. Stepping into that process will equip us to teach others, correct and equip them to do the same.

REVISIT THE TRUTH

> Matthew 6:33—*"But seek first the kingdom of God and his righteousness, and all these things will be added to you."*

Matthew 7:8 *"The one who seeks finds…"*

On this side of Heaven, we will never fully understand everything there is to know about God in all of His Majesty. We have a finite mind trying to understand an infinite God. But we are called to seek Him, to seek His Kingdom and his righteousness. Reading, knowing, memorizing, and teaching His Word to us in scripture is part of that process of seeking God.

The Spirit of God will urge us, speak to us and enable us to go to Him and seek understanding in His Word. The beautiful thing about that process is that it lines up with how the disciples lived. While we have a printed copy of the Word, they walked and talked with the Word. Even in their proximity to the Word, they still needed clarification and repetition to understand the Truths of God. This is why establishing a rhythm of studying and reading the Word is necessary for followers of Christ. It is not a book you can read once and claim full understanding. It is a tool for followers to use to know more of who God is. And when we walk through the process of being in His Word with the goal of knowing Him, he fulfills the promise we see in Matthew 7:7-8. **"Ask, and it will be given to you; seek, and you will find; knock, and it will be opened to you. For everyone who asks receives, and the one who seeks finds, and to the one who knocks it will be opened."**

As we look at how Jesus responded to temptation in the dessert, we should be encouraged to read and know the Bible well. Jesus responded only with Scripture to the lies told by Satan. He did not try to convince Satan of a better way or rationalize what Satan was saying. Jesus knew the Word well enough that He simply responded with truth to combat lies. We should follow the same method when the enemy speaks lies to us.

DO YOU THINK MARY AND JOSEPH LOVED AND RESPECTED JESUS MORE THAN THEIR OTHER KIDS?

PARENT TERMS

Jumping head first into the parenting feels on this question! This one was a little personal than I was ready for that day. I can understand the question about love, but respect…wow! Granted, we were talking about showing respect that day and then the conversation turned to this specific question and I needed to make sure I checked for some layers behind this one.

Please remember to slow down when you hear questions like this. Kids will project your answers over themselves without realizing it. I really had to stop and think about the past few hours and if I had unknowingly shown more love or respect to one of the girls over the others. I didn't want this question being asked out of fear or even confirmation in the child's eyes that we, as parents, simply go back and forth with our love based on behavior from our children. Because the question, "Am I your favorite child" is a constant in life even if it's not voiced directly. The disciples even argued about who was the favorite in Luke 9, 22, and Matthew 18. If it wasn't beyond them to ask, then we can expect our kids to ask too.

Kids are smart! They are also seeking validation and love. So, they know Mary and Joseph were just human parents trying to raise the Savior of the world and probably didn't do it perfectly every time. And we are humans trying to raise little humans and they KNOW we don't do it perfectly!

The answer... Yes, but not really, but also probably, make sense? I believe if Mary and Joseph truly understood who Jesus was (being God and their Savior) then their love for Him would have definitely been different and most likely confusing for them when he was a child. Different doesn't mean that their love was more or less for each child. Mary and Joseph obviously knew Jesus was special and specifically sent from God, hence the virgin birth that almost ended the marriage before it began.

Looking at Luke 2:41-52, Jesus is a young boy and his family has been in Jerusalem for Passover. The family leaves and assumes Jesus is in the large group and they actually walk a day without him. When they got back to Jerusalem, it took them 3 days to find him and they found him in the Temple listening and discussing with the teachers. Mary asked why he treated them like he did and his response was, "why were you looking for me? Did you not know that I must be in my Father's house?" Luke tells us that Mary and Joseph didn't truly understand what He was saying. But His mother treasured those things in her heart as she watched him grow. In that growth, I think their love and respect for Jesus also grew and it grew in a different way than for their other children.

In John 2, when Jesus and His disciples go to the wedding at Cana, it looks like Mary understands who Jesus truly is. She is the one that urges Jesus to do something when the wedding has no more wine. It is like she knows He can do something that no one else can do at that time. Seeing this faith in who Jesus is seems to tell us that Mary had grown in her understanding beyond what the text clearly shows us.

If she (I'd say Joseph too but we don't know if he is still alive at this point), has a clear view that Jesus is not simply a man that she gave birth to but rather that He is the Son of God, then her love and respect for Jesus should be more at this time than for her other children. The respect she had for Jesus would have come from her acknowledgement of His position. Mary might not have fully understood Him as King yet, but we can see a growing understanding by her assumption of His abilities.

That controversial idea of loving God more than family is based on Matthew 10:37 when Jesus says "whoever loves father or mother more than me is not worthy of me, and whoever loves son or daughter more than me is not worthy of me." This is a hard thought to grab ahold of for me. But I believe Jesus is communicating the idea that He must be our priority. If it were to come down to choosing another person over Jesus, even if it is our parent or child, we are called to choose Jesus because no person can be our Savior.

With all that said, does it make more sense that the answer is yes but not really but also probably? Their love and respect for Jesus probably started as a normal parental love would start. It then would have grown as their understanding grew of who Jesus was. This growth in loving Jesus and respecting Him would have been due to who He was before Mary and Joseph were even born. That's why it would have been different than their love for their other children. This doesn't translate to Mary and Joseph loving their other children less. That is another thing the child needs to hear.

Just like Mary and Joseph, we are able to love multiple people in our lives and loving a specific person doesn't take away our love for another. God enables us to love. And Love is not truly limited to a certain number of people. The same is true about respect. Respecting one person doesn't take away from respecting another. But we respect people for different reasons and we respect different positions they hold in life. My love for my wife is different than it is for my children. My love is also the same for each in that I would lay down my life for them all.

KID TERMS

That is a question that a lot of people have when they are parents. I can tell you have thought about this. One great thing about love and respect is that we don't run out of it. If you only have a bag of chips to hand out to people, you will eventually run out. But love and respect aren't like that. We can give as much love and respect to as many people as we meet because God helps us to love.

Loving someone is like truly wanting the best for them and doing what you can to help and protect them. Respecting them is treating them like you want to be treated and putting what they need before what you need. Love and respect kind of overlap and are joined together.

We see in the Bible that Jesus showed us His love by giving His life for us on the cross. The way I show my love to you is that I help provide things for you like food and a home and clothes. I also decided the moment I met you that I would give my life for you if I ever needed to because I want you to have the best life you possibly could have. For Mary and Joseph, they probably loved and respected Jesus a little differently, not really more but different, than His siblings. But that love and respect probably changed when they started to learn more about who Jesus really was and that He would be their savior.

Remember, the great thing about love and respect is that it's not something you run out of.

So, Mary and Joseph could love and respect Jesus differently and still have plenty to love and respect their other kids!

WHY IT'S TRUE

Luke 2:51-52

> [51] *Then he went down to Nazareth with them and was obedient to them. But his mother treasured all these things in her heart.* [52] *And Jesus grew in wisdom and stature, and in favor with God and man.*

As Mary and Joseph raised Jesus, they were given glimpses like this to grow in their understanding of who He was. Their respect and love for Him would have changed over time as God continued to reveal the depth of who their son truly was to them as Lord and Savior.

John 2:1-12

After Mary and Joseph have to go back and find Jesus in the Temple talking with the teachers when He was a young boy, we aren't given any other interactions with His parents. This is estimated to be around 18 years later and Mary seems to have a better understanding of who Jesus is. She doesn't make a specific request of Him, she simply tells Him that they are out of wine before the celebration is over. In those days, that was not a good thing and would have been a disgraceful thing for the family hosting the wedding. But Jesus knew what she wanted of Him by her comment. I think this story shows us Mary's progression in respect of who Jesus was and His position as the Son of God. From the scene in Luke 2 to this interaction we can see that Mary's understanding of what Jesus came to do grew over time.

> 1 John 3:16—*"This is how we know what love is: Jesus Christ laid down his life for us."*

And we ought to lay down our lives for our brothers and sisters. Our example of love is given to us by Jesus. His true sacrifice for us should be how we love others. Love is not quantitative, but rather should be ever flowing from us in how we treat others. Loving someone means you would be willing to give your life over theirs if needed.

REVISIT THE TRUTH

> Matthew 10:37—*"Anyone who loves their father or mother more than me is not worthy of me; anyone who loves their son or daughter more than me is not worthy of me."*

God is pro-family. He created the family with a purpose. Parents are given to children for leadership development, discipleship and to teach them to love. So, this passage can be taken out of context. Jesus is speaking about this commitment required to follow Him and the separation that will come between His followers and those that reject Him. The level of commitment and love for Jesus should be the highest priority of His followers.

As believers grow in understanding of who Jesus is, what they have been saved from, and how Jesus is truly the only source of life available then this desire for God increases. That increase in love and respect toward God will ultimately create a desire to follow and choose God over any other thing or person. This does not mean one should simply leave family and disregard people when they follow God. What this is teaching us is that if a person attempts to pull us away from following God then our choice should be to leave them and follow God.

A young child's understanding of this will be lacking because of the abstract idea of following God. So, we need to help them understand that to follow God over following someone else is to go against what the world wants us to do. We should listen to what God has called us to do; love Him fully and love our neighbor.

GOD + CHURCH—
How God leads
and speaks to
His church

WHY DO WE MAKE BAD CHOICES? (What is Sin?)

PARENT TERMS

This question came at a time that I was very frustrated because of the choice one of the girls had made. So, my heart wanted to just yell, "Because you are a sinner!" Thankfully, I was composed enough not to yell that or even say that directly to my girls.

I want to encourage my girls. I want them to know that I think they are awesome. I don't want anyone to tell them anything different. Every day is a chance for me to express my love to them and emphasize how I see them, how I enjoy them, and how I look forward to being with them.

How I see them as my daughters is different from their standing before God.

Before I can elaborate on the answer to this question, I need them to know they are beautiful, and made in the image of God. But in that image, mankind has brought a "dirtiness" into it all. We each are made in God's image, but SIN has crept into the picture and caused us to have brokenness in our relationship with God.

Man has always had a need for God even before sin entered the picture. But now, our brokenness and broken relationship with God emphasize that need all the more.

That brokenness causes us to do what WE want instead of what God wants us to do in obedience. When we do that, we are telling God that we know what's best for us and that we don't want to listen to Him and his instruction. That is sin. We rebel against God. Essentially, we are claiming to be God and we are ignoring his instruction. This places us in an unrighteous standing before God. We are guilty of sin and deserve the wages or punishment that comes from sin: death (Romans 6:23).

So why do we make bad choices? This question could be answered in two different ways. In light of Romans 7-8, the answers are based on one thing. If the person we are speaking about is not a child of God and has at that point rejected His offering of grace by the death and resurrection of Christ, then that person sins because that is his nature. If we are still living by flesh and have not died to our flesh with Christ, then we will continue to live a life of sin.

If we are a child of God and have been covered by His grace and are declared righteous before God because of the work of Christ, then we sin because we are not walking by faith. We aren't setting our minds on the things of the Spirit, and we aren't listening to the Spirit.

Prior to Jesus returning, believers will continue to have a tension in them with the flesh they are literally in and the Spirit of God in them. A believer has put to death the old self, but the sanctification process of life is when those sinful habits are uprooted out of our minds so we can set our minds on things Above.

The great thing to remember is that we fight this fight from a place of victory. Romans 8 tells us that "There is therefore now no condemnation for those who are in Christ Jesus." Jesus has completed the work for us and has done what we could not do. Sinning less after this point comes from a daily renewal of the mind and submitting to the Spirit as He refines us.

KID TERMS

When Adam and Eve opened the door for sin to enter into this world, every person (except Jesus) born after that came into a broken world with a broken spirit. The thing that is broken inside of us is our "wanter." Our wanter doesn't want to obey God. It wants to do whatever it wants to do, which is usually sin.

And that happens to all of us. Each person needs a savior because we all have sinned. That sin is like being in a boat with a crack in the bottom that gets bigger each day. There's no point in trying to fix it because it can't be fixed. You need a new boat!

That's what happens at salvation. We get a "new boat" or a new self. If we have the new boat but keep trying to jump in the old boat, we won't get where we need to go. And if we don't trust Jesus when he tells us to get in the new boat because our old boat is sinking, then we won't go anywhere and we won't be in a new, unsinkable boat with Jesus.

Plus, this new boat is the perfect boat that can take on water and still never sink! When we are in the new boat, Jesus can show us how to listen to the new "wanter" and stop making those choices.

WHY IT'S TRUE

> Romans 3:23—*"for all have sinned and fall short of the glory of God,"*

We all have sinned and we are broken. There isn't a man born of man (not born of a virgin like Jesus) that isn't born into sin. This means the flesh will always be present on this side of Heaven.

Romans 7-8—A believer lives in victory and when they sin, they do it because they have lost focus on what is ahead and have instead turned back to the old life. The person sinning but without a saving relationship with Christ is living according to the flesh because they are still in their flesh.

REVISIT THE TRUTH

As followers, we must set into motion the rhythms we need in our lives to continuously fight against the flesh that wants nothing more than to lead us astray.

Colossians 1:9–29

This passage brings to light the truth of Christ being fully God and fully man. He is the reason we were created and continue to exist. Knowing Him and knowing more about him is what will strengthen us in the battle against our flesh. As we grow in our knowledge of Christ, we are strengthened, filled with joy, and our focus is directed on Christ and His name rather than on our fleshly desires.

Ephesians 5:1–21

We are given instruction on how to walk by the Spirit and not by the flesh. Temptations will be all around us in this life and our focus should be on the Lord and on bringing things into the Light. Verse 21 points us to a clear focus for our lives to help direct us in how to be imitators of Christ, "submitting to one another out of reverence for Christ." If our focus is not on us, but rather on submitting out of reverence for Christ, walking selflessly by the Spirit will get easier by the day.

Matthew 6:36

If the question comes of what to focus on or how to avoid sin, Jesus speaks to this in the Gospel of Matthew. "Seek first the Kingdom of God and his righteousness," is our focus. We don't need to focus on riches, fame, jobs, or people. We seek Him and He sustains us. We seek Him and He makes everything possible. This passage is at the end of Jesus speaking about not being anxious but rather trusting him to provide. We must trust our Maker and Giver to be all that we need. When we do this, this fight against the flesh is a different story. It's not gone; it's just different than when we allow temptation to sit and give birth to sin in our lives.

Remember, it's not a sin to be tempted. Jesus was tempted. Do we let that temptation sit at our feet and grow roots to become a sin that tries to destroy us? Or do we recognize the temptation for what it is and turn from it and seek His kingdom and righteousness?

WHAT IS A BLESSING?

PARENT TERMS

The technical definition of a "blessing" is the pronouncement of the favor of God on an assembled congregation of persons. More often than not, we see the word blessing refer to material things given to a person or group of people. In the New Testament, we see a blessing as the good that comes from the Gospel. Most people would probably lean toward the material blessing. That idea is most known.

I would say that a blessing could look more like something being removed from a person's life as well as something given to a person. Our perspective of the situation would be the determining factor.

What we see in scripture are references of fathers blessing children, priests blessing people or people being blessed by a gospel message. Scripture even shows us prayers asking God to bless food prior to eating it.

Personally, I have seen God take a job opportunity away and that was a blessing. At the time, it didn't seem like it with no other job lined up. But it opened the door for the next opportunity. He can also allow people to leave your life and it might feel painful at the time, but God could see that as a blessing as He gives you another friendship or relationship that brings Him glory.

Ultimately, a blessing is something good given or pronounced over someone and it is from God. It is not man-made. It is directly from the Lord. And the blessing isn't always one specific thing. For instance, finding wood could be a blessing if you need to build a fire to stay warm. Finding wood in your hand as a splinter, that's not a blessing. It's the same thing but not always a blessing. The intent of the material helps define the blessing.

KID TERMS

One awesome thing we know about blessings is that they are from God. God gives his people blessings for his glory. Sometimes those blessings are things like houses and sometimes they could be thoughts or jobs or relationships or a blessing could be money. One important thing to remember is that not everyone is blessed with the same thing. And a blessing to one person might not be a blessing to another person.

Most would think that a blessing is something given to us. But a blessing could also be something that is taken out of our lives, either for a time or forever. We don't always know what is best for us and there are times when God needs to remove things for us to see what He is doing in our lives.

We also can't just say "more is better" or that one specific thing is always a blessing. A piece of wood could be a great thing! If we need to build a fire, it's great to have. If it's a tiny piece of wood that somehow gets in our skin (splinter) then it's NOT a good thing!

So, blessings aren't just things or people given or taken away from our lives. Blessings deal more with opportunities in our lives to glorify God.

WHY IT'S TRUE

> Matthew 14:19—"*Then he ordered the crowds to sit down on the grass, and taking the five loaves and the two fish, he looked up to heaven and said a blessing. Then he broke the loaves and gave them to the disciples, and the disciples gave them to the crowds.*"

Jesus asked the Father to bless the loaves and fish for multiplication. The small amount of food is a blessing because no one else had food. Jesus is asking the Father to bless it even more.

Deuteronomy 33:1 "This is the blessing with which Moses the man of God blessed the people of Israel before his death."

Moses blesses for each tribe of Israel before his death that walks through how God will use and bless each tribe. The blessings speak highly of how God will use them for His glory.

> Romans 15:29 *"I know that when I come to you I will come in the fullness of the blessing of Christ."*

Paul uses the phrase "blessing of Christ" in this passage. Commentators believe this can be expounded into the idea of "the rich blessings from Christ" or even the "full measure of the Gospel." Paul is speaking about bringing a blessing that is from The Lord that is not a simple possession that Paul would bring. It is a powerful blessing that will bless the Romans fully.

> James 3:10—*"From the same mouth come blessing and cursing. My brothers, these things ought not to be so."*

James is proclaiming the truth of our actions in faith. Our faith is shown by our actions and James is saying that truth and lies shouldn't come from the same source just as salt water and fresh water cannot come from the same source. Blessings and cursing have no place together.

REVISIT THE TRUTH

In Genesis 12, God calls Abram to follow him and he will make Abram a blessing to the world. We need to understand that this blessing overflows to us. God's people should be a blessing to the world. We should proclaim the truth of who Jesus is and the truth of his life, death, and resurrection. How we live should be a blessing to everyone. The children of God are not called to be a burden in this world but rather a complete blessing. And that only happens by way of the Spirit working in us.

James 3:10 "From the same mouth come blessing and cursing. My brothers, these things ought not to be so." Our mouths should bring that blessing of the Gospel. How can a blessing and curse come from the same mouth? How can salt water and fresh water come from the same source?

As we speak, we must remember our calling as a blessing to the nations. Every word and action are observed and scrutinized. So, when we are blessed, we should see that blessing as a way for us to bless others. Ultimately, everything we have belongs to God and we are stewarding it. That includes our mouths and the words we speak.

HOW DOES GOD TALK TO US?

PARENT TERMS

We get to pray. God has made it possible for us to have a conversation with him. Sometimes we forget that a conversation involves talking and listening. So, when we do go to God in prayer, we need to spend time waiting for a response. We see Christ take time every morning to go be alone with the Father. In the Garden, we see Christ pleading with the Father. The Psalms are filled with prayers to God. Some of those prayers are laments, some prayers are praises, and some are pleading with God for direction or even asking if God is still present. Our prayers are a key part of our relationship with God.

God uses His Word to communicate His truth. He used prophets in the past to communicate to his people and to the church in the future. If we spend time reading His word and listening, then he will speak to our hearts. It does take practice to know if the "groanings" we get are from God or from our own hearts wanting something in our flesh. We can put whatever thought or feeling we have next to what the Bible says about God and how he has interacted in the past to see if it lines up. As we read through His Word, we need to be careful not to pull out specific things to justify what we are questioning or desiring to do. He speaks through His word with proper exegesis (proper critical explanation or interpretation of a text) and not "eisegesis" which focuses on the "I" to have God talk to us how we see fit.

God will speak through people in our lives as well. The hope is that you are reading this to be one of those people for a child by answering a question about God or the bible. We should surround ourselves with people that are going to speak God's Truth to us and encourage us to place what they say up against what the Bible says to solidify and confirm what is taught.

One key element to remember when God speaks to us is that we are called to listen. In John 10:27 Jesus says, "My sheep hear my voice, and I know them, and they follow me." It's one thing to hear God, but it's another step to hear it and follow it. It takes time for us to hear His voice and listen well enough to distinguish it from all the other voices in the world. Be encouraged because God will continue to talk to you so that you will know His voice.

KID TERMS

We have a few ways that God speaks to us.

The most personal way is in prayer. We can sit and talk with God whenever we want. We can speak it out loud, to ourselves, or even write it down. If you want to get really creative, you can sing your prayers like we see in the Psalms. We can also sit and listen for God to respond. You probably won't hear a voice like you do when talking with your friends, but God definitely speaks to our hearts. It's almost like a whisper to our hearts. It could even be something like an idea that just keeps coming to your thoughts and someone you trust brings it up to you, too.

God also gave us his Word! We can spend time with Him by reading the Bible and learning more about Him and His truths. The Bible can speak to us every day if we spend time in it and listen for the Spirit to teach us. There are times when a certain verse will just stop us in our tracks when we are reading. Those can be times when God is using the Bible to speak to us.

The third way God speaks to us is through people we trust in our lives. That could be Mom and Dad, a teacher, a pastor, or anyone we know who loves Jesus. God uses so many people in our lives to teach His truths and we still get to take what we hear from them and pray about it and put it next to what the Bible says to make sure it's true.

WHY IT'S TRUE

> Luke 19:46—*"saying to them, "It is written, 'My house shall be a house of prayer,' but you have made it a den of robbers."'*

The church is called to be a house of prayer. Followers of Christ have the Spirit dwelling inside of them therefore followers are the church body, a house, and should be a house of prayer. The structure of a believer's life should be formed by prayer.

Throughout Psalms (86, 88 to name a couple) the psalmist pleads for God to hear his prayer. We should constantly go to the Lord in prayer for all things. It doesn't matter the size of prayer or the amount of big theological words.

> John 1:14—*"And the Word became flesh and dwelt among us"*

John tells us that the Word of God became flesh and dwelt among us. This Word, Christ, is the power behind the written word given to us. He is the word. So, spending time in the Word is spending time knowing Him.

Proverbs 27:17 teaches us that "Iron sharpens iron as one man sharpens another." We are called to sharpen one another. Sharpening something usually involves a rough process of removing small pieces along the way. In Titus, Paul even instructs the older men to disciple and teach younger men and the same for older women to younger women. This is how the Gospel message moves from one generation to another.

REVISIT THE TRUTH

1 Thessalonians 5:17—Paul writes to "pray without ceasing." That might seem like an unattainable task. And it is unattainable with the mindset that prayer is only sitting down with eyes closed and heads bowed. But prayer is more of a posture of the heart than a physical posture. Physical posture can help you focus in prayer, but it's not necessary. Children of God should be in a state of mind that communication with God throughout the day is as regular as starting a conversation with the person next to you. It can happen whenever you want and with any surrounding chaos. The idea of "without ceasing" can also help you understand that you should always be ready to speak with him, either alone or possibly with someone near you at the time.

WHY DO WE GIVE MONEY TO THE CHURCH?

PARENT TERMS

I'm so glad my kids asked this question because it shows they are paying attention and they are understanding, or at least are curious, about how the church functions. My background is vocational ministry and so that means my salary was only possible due to people being obedient and giving a tithe to the church body. This answer is not to offer a quick response for debate on whether or not ministers should make tons of money. Lord knows I never did on church staff. This question should yield an answer that takes us through steps of obedience and spiritual growth.

We give to the church because we believe that some people are called to be paid through the church for their work. In 1 Corinthians 9:13-14 it says "Do you not know that those who are employed in the temple service get their food from the temple, and those who serve at the altar share in the sacrificial offerings? In the same way, the Lord commanded that those who proclaim the gospel should get their living by the gospel."

Paul gives us an example of giving so that some can make their living from the work of the Gospel. We know that Paul didn't only make his living from the church body. During his time in Corinth (Acts 18:3) he spent time as a tentmaker and spent his time reasoning in the synagogue every Sabbath. Solely living off money given to the church seems to be seasonal for Paul.

We also don't want to tell people how much we tithe. It's not about who gives the most. It's about being faithful and trusting God to be faithful in how he provides and uses what is already His.

In Luke 21:1-4 the Bible tells the story of a widow giving a small gift in secret compared to rich people giving much publicly. This story of the widow's offering is evidence that people should bring what they have in faith, and it is clear to followers to not be boastful of the amount given. The heart is the indicator of amount and quality. This same truth is evident in the story of Cain and Abel in Genesis 4. Cain simply brought some of his crop and not the first fruits and best. Abel brings an offering of the firstborn in his flock.

The New Testament actually doesn't stress the same 10% command given in the Old Testament, but truly stresses giving from what you have and being prayerful about giving out of your abundance. In 2 Corinthians 8:1-15 it doesn't say NOT to give, but rather to focus on your heart and the JOY of giving and taking part in what God is doing through his church.

This could also lead to the question "Can we give more than the 10%?" and of course the answer is YES! There have been several times that the Lord has pressed upon our hearts and other believers to go beyond the minimum. Some see that as something different. You could place "tithe" under the 10% and beyond that is an "offering" as mentioned in Luke 21:1-4.

FOR OLDER KIDS—If your child knows about taxes and money matters, they might wonder about whether we should calculate a 10% tithe before taxes or after? I believe that tithing BEFORE taxes is the biblical standard because God wants our first fruits, not leftovers. That discussion could then lead into budgeting and its spiritual ramifications

KID TERMS

One of the unique things about our money is that it isn't really our money. God wants us to give a certain amount (tithe) to the church from the "first fruits," (Proverbs 3:9) meaning when we first get money. You see, it all belongs to God and He lets us use it (we call it stewarding). That's why Mommy and Daddy believe we should pray about how we spend our money. God wants us to set aside 10% (like if I gave you $10, you'd give $1 or 10%) and then God says live faithfully on the rest of it. Some people think that's hard to do, but if we trust in

God's faithfulness to provide and we live like the first $1 always goes to God's church for ministry, then we just live like we make $9 instead of $10.

We do this for a couple of great reasons. We are obedient to what God has called us to do. We want to live like all we have belongs to God because He provided it all. We just get to use it. We want to provide for others. We trust that the church body we give to uses that money to do a few different things.

The church pays the ministers on staff, the church pays for buildings or specific ministry tools. The church also gives money away to others that are partners in sharing about Jesus and His Love. So instead of us trying to find all the different places to divide up our money, we trust the ministers of the church to send the money to those that need it. We get to give to the church because God chose to use the church to impact and change the world.

WHY IT'S TRUE

> 1 Corinthians 9:14—"*In the same way, the Lord commanded that those who proclaim the gospel should get their living by the gospel.*"

We are given clear instruction to pay some that can make their entire living by way of preaching the Gospel. It doesn't say if that should be a large amount and it definitely doesn't say it should be a small amount. It gives instruction that they should be able to make a living with it.

> 2 Corinthians 8:1-15—"We want you to know, brothers, about the grace of God that has been given among the churches of Macedonia, **2** for in a severe test of affliction, their abundance of joy and their extreme poverty have overflowed in a wealth of generosity on their part. **3** For they gave according to their means, as I can testify, and beyond their means, of their own accord, **4** begging us earnestly for the favor of taking part in the relief of the saints—**5** and this, not as we expected, but they gave themselves first to the Lord and then by the will of God to us. **6** Accordingly, we urged Titus that as he had started, so he should complete among you this act of grace. **7** But as you excel in everything—in faith, in speech, in knowledge, in all earnestness, and in our love for you—see that you excel in this act of grace also.
>
> **8** I say this not as a command, but to prove by the earnestness of others that your love also is genuine. **9** For you know the grace of our Lord Jesus Christ, that though he was rich,

yet for your sake he became poor, so that you by his poverty might become rich. **10** And in this matter I give my judgment: this benefits you, who a year ago started not only to do this work but also to desire to do it. **11** So now finish doing it as well, so that your readiness in desiring it may be matched by your completing it out of what you have. **12** For if the readiness is there, it is acceptable according to what a person has, not according to what he does not have. **13** For I do not mean that others should be eased and you burdened, but that as a matter of fairness **14** your abundance at the present time should supply their need, so that their abundance may supply your need, that there may be fairness. **15** As it is written, "Whoever gathered much had nothing left over, and whoever gathered little had no lack."

Paul is encouraging the church to look for those in need. He reminds them that there will be time that each of them will have a need and the church can supply those needs. He isn't calling for them to give away all of their money. He simply wants them to be willing to give what they have to those in need, trusting that the same grace will be shown to them.

Acts 18:3—*"and because he was of the same trade he stayed with them and worked, for they were tentmakers by trade."*

Paul did not always ask for all his needs to be met by way of the church. He knew a trade and would earn money making tents during longer stays on his journeys.

REVISIT THE TRUTH

In 2 Corinthians 8:1-15 Paul tells of the generosity of the churches of Macedonia. He writes about how they gave beyond what anyone expected. They were poor but they desired and begged to be "a part in the relief of the saints." It seems as though Paul did not even try to take their gifts, but they insisted so that they could be a part of the movement of the Gospel to others that they would most likely never meet. Their poverty increased by earthly standards so their joy in sharing in the Gospel could increase!

Paul doesn't speak of a new commandment to give in such a way that one's poverty increases. He does urge the readers to understand that they should ready themselves in desiring the same heart as the churches of Macedonia. Paul also urges them to recognize the giving spirit of the poor that are mentioned and see their own wealth as a way to give to them and bless their obedience to the Lord.

Pray that your heart stays ready to give everything if called for the sake of the Gospel. That calling may never come and it might come more than once. God desires for us to prepare our hearts for what He has created for us to do.

WHAT DID THEY DO DIFFERENTLY IN THE OT AND NT?

PARENT TERMS

This question was mainly aimed at worship and what church gathering time looked like in the Old Testament versus the New Testament shortly after Jesus ascended into Heaven.

The Old Testament system was centered on the sacrificial system that the priests were strictly commanded to follow. We can even read about priests that thought they could do it better and changed things up and they died because of it in Leviticus 10:1-2.

These priests' clothing was even special and set apart for the sacrificial system. They were given specific instructions on what to wear, how to wear it and when they could present the offerings. They needed to be exact on how they prepared the offerings and even give offerings for their own sin prior to presenting for Israel so they could go before the Lord blameless. This was a constant, repetitious ceremony that they were commanded to do in order that they might have communion with God through the priesthood.

Things changed after the crucifixion of Christ.

One of the major elements in the Old Testament worship was the veil that surrounded the Holy of Holies. It was made of beautiful blue and purple and scarlet yarns with cherubim sewn into it. It was hung on large golden hooks off of four large pillars (Exodus 26:31–33). This veil was to protect God's people from the presence of God. God knew his people had to be separated from Him due to their sin and His holiness. Sin cannot be in the presence of a holy God.

Prior to Christ coming to earth, only the high priest could go behind the curtain and the Temple was the only place for sacrifices on the altar. Christ completes the sacrificial system by being the perfect sacrifice. He died once for all. Christ's death and resurrection fulfilled the curse of the law and mankind could all come before God by way of His redemption. At the time of Jesus' death on the cross, the veil in the temple is torn from top to bottom. That was significant in that it shows the opening of the Holy of Holies was completed from above and not done by man. That was a sign that God was inviting all people into His presence.

The bigger picture of what was different had to do with the law as well. The law's purpose was not for Israel to follow perfectly, but rather to show

Israel her sin and lacking when it came to the holiness of God. The intention of creation was for mankind to live in obedience to God, but mankind wasn't able to do that due to sin.

We needed the perfect sacrifice of Jesus on the cross to fulfill the law and the need for atonement (big word for payment) for sin. Without Jesus' sacrifice, God's people would continue in the sacrificial system. Jesus even speaks of the transition away from worship being bound to a singular place when speaking with the woman at the well in John 4.

She tells Jesus that the Jews have instructed them that the only place to worship is in Jerusalem. Jesus responds with, "Woman, believe me, the hour is coming when neither on this mountain nor in Jerusalem will you worship the Father." The act of worship was to be done at the place where God's presence rested, the Temple. But Jesus sends the Spirit to dwell in His children so true worship can happen anywhere.

KID TERMS

After Adam and Eve let sin come into the world, people didn't get to just spend time with God like before. The relationship was broken and mankind was full of sin. This meant that in order for a person to go before God and worship, he would need to be cleansed of the sin. This was to protect that person from the punishment of God for that sin. So, God created a temporary way for mankind to still come into His presence and worship Him.

He chose some men to be priests. And these priests followed a ton of rules given by God to prepare themselves to take what's called an offering to God for the sin of people. They had to do the same thing over and over again because people continue to sin.

But in the New Testament, God changed some things. Technically, we could say things changed after the resurrection of Jesus in the New Testament. God sent Jesus to be the perfect sacrifice that no other priest could present. Jesus' perfect sacrifice of himself was the last offering needed to pay for the sins of God's people. This opened the door for us to go to God whenever we want to worship and bring offerings of praise. So, the big difference is that we have more of a personal relationship with God that frees us to worship Him anywhere.

WHY IT'S TRUE

Hebrews 4:14-5:10—**14** "Since then we have a great high priest who has passed through the heavens, Jesus, the Son of God, let us hold fast our confession. **15** For we do not have a high priest who is unable to sympathize with our weaknesses, but one who in every respect has been tempted as we are, yet without sin.

16 Let us then with confidence draw near to the throne of grace, that we may receive mercy and find grace to help in time of need.

5:1 For every high priest chosen from among men is appointed to act on behalf of men in relation to God, to offer gifts and sacrifices for sins. **2** He can deal gently with the ignorant and wayward, since he himself is beset with weakness. **3** Because of this he is obligated to offer sacrifice for his own sins just as he does for those of the people. **4** And no one takes this honor for himself, but only when called by God, just as Aaron was.

5 So also Christ did not exalt himself to be made a high priest, but was appointed by him who said to him,

"You are my Son, today I have begotten you";

6 as he says also in another place, "You are a priest forever, after the order of Melchizedek."

7 In the days of his flesh, Jesus offered up prayers and supplications, with loud cries and tears, to him who was able to save him from death, and he was heard because of his reverence. **8** Although he was a son, he learned obedience through what he suffered. **9** And being made perfect, he became the source of eternal salvation to all who obey him, **10** being designated by God a high priest after the order of Melchizedek."

We see Jesus as the high priest that is able to present himself without blemish to be the ultimate sacrifice and offering to God for payment of sin.

> Mark 15:38— *"And the curtain of the temple was torn in two, from top to bottom."*

The Temple veil is torn in two, from top to bottom. This happens as Jesus is dying on the cross and is not done by man but rather by God. God is opening the door for His people to come into His presence like never before.

Romans 5:8-9—"but God shows his love for us in that while we were still sinners, Christ died for us. Since, therefore, we have now been justified by his blood, much more shall we be saved by him from the wrath of God."—Jesus is the payment for our sin and the reason we will not experience the wrath of God at judgment and can go before God confidently if we are His redeemed children.

REVISIT THE TRUTH

Romans 3:21-31 "**21** But now the righteousness of God has been manifested apart from the law, although the Law and the Prophets bear witness to it—**22** the righteousness of God through faith in Jesus Christ for all who believe. For there is no distinction: **23** for all have sinned and fall short of the glory of God, **24** and are justified by his grace as a gift, through the redemption that is in Christ Jesus, **25** whom God put forward as a propitiation by his blood, to be received by faith. This was to show God's righteousness, because in his divine forbearance he had passed over former sins. **26** It was to show his righteousness at the present time, so that he might be just and the justifier of the one who has faith in Jesus.

27 Then what becomes of our boasting? It is excluded. By what kind of law? By a law of works? No, but by the law of faith.**28** For we hold that one is justified by faith apart from works of the law. **29** Or is God the God of Jews only? Is he not the God of Gentiles also? Yes, of Gentiles also, **30** since God is one—

> who will justify the circumcised by faith and the uncircumcised through faith. **31** Do we then overthrow the law by this faith? By no means! On the contrary, we uphold the law.

Paul is writing on the righteousness of God through faith. The Old Testament spoke of man repeating the necessary sacrifices and continuous repentance for a temporary time before God. Christ dying on the cross and faith in Him bestows the righteousness of God on believers. This means the law is fulfilled and is the means by which God allows a person to come before Him. We all have sinned and we continue to sin. But the death and resurrection of Christ covers those sins and forever declares his children righteous before God. God does not simply ignore the sins of believers, but rather He placed His wrath for judgment of those sins on His Son on the cross. That opened the door for believers to come before God in a redemptive relationship, having no need for more sacrifices, which is physically shown in the torn veil at the temple.

DO WE STILL HAVE TO FOLLOW THE 10 COMMANDMENTS PERFECTLY?

PARENT TERMS

If you read through the Old Testament with your kids, this question will come up. It is still a question asked by so many adults today, and that is okay. These types of questions are beneficial to our faith because they attempt to bring understanding of who God is. The obvious underlayer of these questions is linked to truths known in the Old Testament like grace and mercy.

From my experience, this question or one like it from an adult is sprinkled with a hint of "gotcha" tone. The asker is wanting to hear something that would negate all things Old Testament or even New Testament, based on your answer. The idea behind that tone is that if the 10 commandments are out, then all the other commandments go with it unless specifically commanded by someone in the New Testament. It's basically the "Jesus didn't say it" argument.

Hearing this question from your child doesn't really bring that same tone. It is truly a question to try and bring some kind of bridge between the Old Testament law and the cross in the New Testament. The beautiful thing about the answer is that Jesus is literally that bridge between the Testaments.

To answer the question, it's a yes but also a no. When we read through Romans 3, we see that the law can only justify someone if it is followed perfectly. But we have all sinned and fallen short, so the law is not something that brings righteousness on us. It reflects our sin. In the same breath (it might have been the same breaths because Paul just seems to do run on after run on after run on… you get it) Paul reminds us that it is by faith we are justified.

Should we throw the law out? Verse 31 "by no means!" We are still called to live according to the law. This is where that "yes" comes into play. We follow the law and strive toward the perfection it illuminates in the midst of our sanctification (process of being made holy) but remember that we are not saved by works but rather by faith. That is how Jesus becomes that bridge between the Old and New. The law is given, men strive for perfection, and never reach it. Jesus comes and lives a perfect life following God's law perfectly and dies the death we deserve for failing to follow the law perfectly. Then He bestows His righteousness upon us as followers in the faith that His death on the cross and resurrection from the grave is the payment for our sins.

To sum up: No, we don't follow the commandments for salvation, but, yes, we follow out of obedience to God. Jesus followed them perfectly for us. As followers of Christ, we get to have the righteousness from His perfection cover us.

KID TERMS

One of the main things we need to know about the 10 commandments is that they were given to God's people to point them to Jesus. God wanted His people to know that He requires perfection (no sin) to have a relationship with Him. And the Law gave us the plans for how someone could live a perfect life. The bad part is that no one other than Jesus could live that perfect life.

So, God wanted His people to follow the Law out of love and obedience with the faith that God would provide the ultimate sacrifice needed to pay for sin. That sacrifice is Jesus. He lived perfectly, died in our place, and rose from the grave. His death was the last sacrifice needed to pay for sin that came from breaking the 10 commandments. But that doesn't mean we throw the law out the window because we are shown grace and mercy by God. It's not just a set of rules. They point us to see how Jesus lived and our need for Him. He still wants us to try and follow the commandments out of love and obedience to him.

WHY IT'S TRUE

Romans 3, 6, 7, 8

These passages show us our lacking when it comes to perfection. We all have fallen short of the glory of God (Rom 3:23) and we all were under the curse of the law. The law was given to show us God's expectations and to give us a clearer picture of who God is in his holiness. God does not change or correct himself. The law wasn't just erased when Jesus died on the cross. The law was fulfilled and completed through his sacrifice. This should be a driving force behind us desiring to follow the commands of God. The law does not save us, but our faith in Christ fulfilling the law is our saving grace. We then get to live in victory (Rom 8) without condemnation because of His saving grace!

REVISIT THE TRUTH

Romans 6 is such a great picture of our status with God through Christ. We die with Christ to sin (the curse of the Law), and we live with Christ and because of his death once for all and his resurrection, we know that death has no power over him or us as his children. The law points us to the perfection needed to be in the family of God. That perfection is granted to us through the death of Christ and his resurrection which places the power over death on our lives. Our physical bodies will still die, and we should live in such a way as to flee from our fleshly passions. But we are no longer under the law and sin has no power over us. The law can be a heavy burden if one believes they must live it perfectly. That is why Christ did it for us and gave us victory in Him!

www.ingramcontent.com/pod-product-compliance
Lightning Source LLC
LaVergne TN
LVHW051241080426
835513LV00016B/1710